HOW TO RAISE PARENTS

HOW TO RAISE PARENTS

Questions and Answers for Teens and Parents

CLAYTON C. BARBEAU

1817

HARPER & ROW, PUBLISHERS, SAN FRANCISCO

Cambridge, Hagerstown, New York, Philadelphia, Washington
London, Mexico City, São Paulo, Singapore, Sydney

FIRST EDITION

Designed by Donald Hatch

Library of Congress Cataloging-in-Publication Data

Barbeau, Clayton C.
  How to raise parents.

  Bibliography: p.
  Summary: Advice for helping teenagers and parents get
through the teen years. Includes chapters on divorce,
drugs, the blues, sexuality, and schoolwork.
    1. Adolescence—Miscellanea. 2. Youth—Miscellanea.
3. Parent and child—Miscellanea. [1. Adolescence.
2. Parent and child] I. Title.
HQ796.B274 1987   646.7'8   86–42988
ISBN 0–06–250044–9

---

87 88 89 90 91 HC 10 9 8 7 6 5 4 3 2 1

To Michael Conrad (1955–   )
Amy Elizabeth (1956–   )
Rose-Marie (1958–   )
Margaret Ann (1960–   )
Mark Jerome (1961–   )
Daniel Joseph (1963–   )
Jennifer Irene (1965–   )
Christopher Charles (1967–   )
who raised me up; and

To Myra Ellen (1931–1979),
their mother,
whom death took from us,
but who is very much alive in us all.

Contents

Acknowledgments

First, to my son, Christopher Charles, now nineteen, who read the manuscript and offered suggestions that helped;

To Paul Bunning, who helped sort the questions, ask them, and cut the fat out of my answers, truly a facilitator, and Ed and Gloria Coker, friends as well as agents;

To Maureen Lenihan, for encouragement and helpful suggestions;

To the thousands of young people who've shared their pain and their laughter with me and graced me with their trust and openness;

And to all those who asked me to do this work:

Thanks

Preface

One evening some years ago I spoke to students at the University of Washington in Seattle. It was final exam week, and after I finished, around 10:30, I said, "Well, that's it." But nobody left.

I said, "I know you have exams," but still they stayed. Finally, at 12:30 A.M., I said to about fifteen students still gathered around me, "It's obvious everyone's waiting to talk to me individually. Why don't we make it a group session? Who wants to be brave enough to go first?"

The first questioner asked, "How do you cut the umbilical cord?" Another said, "Yeah, my mother's crying all the time." Another chimed in, "My father thinks I've really run out on him by going away to college."

The next day I was in Yakima, Washington, to address a conference of educators and parents on "Contemporary Youth: A Challenge to Parents." When I came into the room I told the crowd I wanted to share with them the dialogue of the night before. I quoted, "How do we encourage them to stand on their own two feet? How do we tell them they can do it? That they've got to be able to make it on their own? Because when we cut the umbilical cord it's really traumatic for them."

Parents in the room nodded their heads sagely, thinking I was quoting parents. When I told them college kids had expressed these thoughts, they were astonished.

I announced I was retitling my talk "Contemporary Parents: A Challenge to Youth."

When I finished my remarks a teenaged girl stood and said, "I came in by accident. I don't think I'm supposed to be here, but everything you said applies to me!" Weeping, she blurted out a story of the pain she had been feeling as she tried to get her parents to let go.

The next day I was strolling among the conference exhibits when I spotted a girl of about seventeen at one of the booths. I sat down and shared a brownie with her. I told her I was going to talk to parents later that day and asked her what she thought I should say. She answered, "You've got to tell them to talk to us! Every time I try to get my mother to talk to me she says, 'Clean your room' or 'Go to the store for me' or 'Empty the garbage' or 'Have you done your homework?' I don't want to tell her how to raise me, but it's very important that we have a discussion pretty soon so we can understand each other, or there'll be a big explosion!"

That's why I've written this book based on the questions teenagers have asked me during my travels around the country. It is the kind of discussion I hope will help teenagers and their parents understand each other and perhaps even stop a few big explosions.

Whether we are parents or teenagers we must remember family life is a collaboration. Some young people tend to see family life as a one-way street, with their parents as solely responsible for the creation of the family. These same young people are rightfully seeking, as they mature, more freedom to exercise choice in their lives. Teenagers, as well as parents, must understand they share in the creation of the quality of their family life.

1

On Helping Parents
Be Independent

1

How can I raise my parents? They already are who they are.

The very advent of a baby transforms a husband and wife into father and mother. Your parents were created as parents on the day you were conceived; they became father and mother of a new being in the world. Even before you were born, they had to start meeting your needs. You were already creating them in a new fashion, changing their lives radically. People who never got up at two in the morning now were getting up to feed you.

People who had total freedom to choose how to spend their evenings, mornings, Saturdays, or Sundays now had to ask, "What'll we do about the baby?"

They became concerned about the future in a new way. Suddenly, they cared about the school system; they cared in a new way about where the country was going, where the world was going.

They became more involved in the future because you would be living in the future. So, right up to this day, up to the time you're reading this page, you have been raising your parents to new levels of awareness.

As an infant you were unaware of your impact, but today as an adolescent you can consciously shape the quality of your relationship with your parents. You can help them in parenting; you can share the burden by taking on more responsibility for yourself and the family.

So you think I have the power to do all that?

Yes. It's very likely you underestimate your influence on your family. If you are loving, you create a different family than if you are angry. If you act sullen and hide in your room, your family is different than when you are cheerful and cooperative. If you hide your feelings, your parents won't know how to approach you.

Even if you have parents with problems—and many kids do—(28 million young people in this country are being raised by one or more alcoholic parents, for example), you can help solve the problems rather than just sitting back and being resentful. (I'll tell you how a little later.)

Half the kids in America will be living in a single-parent home by the time they are eighteen. You may already be among the one out of five young people with only one parent in your home. If so, your parent may not have anyone with whom to share parental responsibilities. If divorced, your parent may feel he or she has failed in a major area of life. Your attitude counts a lot in these situations.

Many parents yearn to be patted on the back by their kids and told, "I think you're doing a good job." If you come home and give Mom a kiss or Dad a hug and say, "Gee, it's good to be here," or "Hey, I think you're doing a great job Mom (or Dad)," you might boost morale enormously.

Even if your parents are not ideal, you can still help them by showing understanding, creativity. Your attitude is very important to their emotional lives and the emotional climate of your family.

Maybe this is a dumb question, but what are adolescents? And why is it so hard to be one?

It's not a dumb question. In fact, adolescence is a time full of questions; the questions are not only not dumb but tend to be among the most important in the world simply *because* they are asked in adolescence.

Some people confuse *adolescence* and *puberty,* as if these terms mean the same thing. They don't.

Puberty begins between the ages of nine and eleven, depending on whether you are a boy or a girl, and ends around sixteen to eighteen. It's basically a physical and hormonal process.

Your soft baby skin becomes thicker and more oily. That's why about 70 percent of young people will have skin problems. Your baby jaw will be moving forward to take its adult shape, and this may temporarily affect your eardrums —and that means the stereo gets played louder. Parents will yell, "Are you deaf?" and the answer, in puberty, is, "Yes, partially."

Hair is thickening and growing in strange places. The word *puberty* comes from the Latin *pubescere,* which means "to get hairy." In fact, puberty is a very hairy time. At least seven powerful hormones are being shot through your body, chiefly testosterone in boys and estrogen in girls. These chemicals cause dramatic emotional shifts—real highs and real lows. Suicidal depression can be followed by a wonderfully exhilarating mood. That's one reason it is particularly stupid to take drugs at this time: your body is producing all of its own mood-altering chemicals. Pubescents have natural highs.

These shifts from gloom to delight and back again can be

as bewildering to you as to anybody around you.

Testosterone and estrogen are both sex hormones, so puberty also means sexy feelings are arising and sexual changes are taking place. The boy's body is preparing for fatherhood, for the production of fertile semen, and he is having erections, usually at embarrassing times. The girl's body is preparing for motherhood, and she is entering her menarche, her first time of menstruation, and her body is regulating its cycle.

I don't want to get too clinical about this, but that's what puberty is: a time we grow up enough physically to have children of our own.

Adolescence, on the other hand, is the time when you are meant to be asking yourself the major questions of life. In adolescence you ask: "Who am I?" "Who are all these people I live with?" "What am I doing on earth?" "What on earth am I doing here?"

It's the time to ask: "What are my talents?" "What do I look like compared with the people around me?" "How do they see me?" "How do I see myself?" "How do I feel about myself?"

You ask about spiritual values, too: "How do I relate to God?" "Do I believe in God?" "What does my religion mean?" "What are my values in life?" "What are my goals?" "How do I achieve my goals?"

And, finally, you might even ask, "What do I want on my tombstone?"

These are very important questions. The task of adolescence is to answer them. When you have found the answers, you'll also find that you naturally will be "paying your own bills" financially, emotionally, and spiritually.

So long as you are dependent upon your parents in any one of those ways, you are still an adolescent.

In our culture we have been extending adolescence; there was a time when adolescence was finished by the age of fourteen at the latest. Most people were out in the workforce paying their own bills, meeting their own needs, living independently from their parents by that age.

In the early days of industrialization, children as young as five worked from thirteen to sixteen hours a day in sweatshops, mills, factories, and mines. Religious and political leaders approved of this exploitation for they considered "idle hands—the devil's tools." In England in 1878 the minimum age for full-time employment was set at ten. In the U.S., young boys and girls were employed in even the most hazardous occupations. The cotton mills advertised for workers—specifically boys and girls "8 to 12" years of age.

It was Massachusetts which in 1842 adopted a law limiting the work day for children under twelve to only ten hours per day. Early in this century twenty percent of the children in the U.S. were wage earners. Charles Dickens's "Oliver Twist" is less fiction than fact in its tale of young persons of 100 years ago trying to survive.

All that ended with the child labor laws in the 1940s. Today, some people expect their parents to pay their bills, financially and otherwise, right through college.

If, during this crucial period, you avoid looking hard at questions of "Who am I?" and "What do I want to do with my life?" you may find yourself at the age of thirty, or forty, going through a delayed adolescence. Some of my clients in therapy are married and have children of their own, but they actually demolish their family in order to pose the questions they should have answered by the age of twenty-one or twenty-two or twenty-three. "I must find myself," they say.

Choices made in adolescence have long range consequences, which is why it's a scary time. You may make some wrong choices, maybe some large mistakes—that's part of being human—but how you handle your choices and, yes, how you respond to your successes and your mistakes at this time will have a lot to do with the quality of your life for years to come.

Add puberty to adolescence, and it's easy to see why this is one of the most stressful times in your life. Few adults would choose to relive it.

The adolescence you talk about scares me! How can I do all that? It just makes me want to run away.

One way you can run away is by abusing alcohol or drugs, but they only fragment you further and don't resolve the basic questions. Running away causes larger problems and can even destroy your chance for a good and satisfying life.

Some teenagers try to answer the questions of adolescence by rushing into premature sex. Deep inside, they believe, "If I cling to this other person I won't have to answer, 'Who am I?' " Yes, your sexual partner may seem to tell you you're lovable—for a while. But at the very time you should be putting yourself together, you'd be giving yourself away. You'd be keeping yourself from meeting all kinds of other people who can help teach you who you are.

Based on my therapy with adolescents—both teenagers and forty year olds—I'm convinced you would do well to be friends with as many persons of the opposite sex as you can before you're out of high school. Likewise, involving yourself in school activities—student government, the newspaper, the band, the science club, athletics—and sharing in group activities exposes you to a lot of different people off whom to bounce your personality and you gain a sense of your own attractiveness and develop your social poise.

That's part of your education too. Don't make the mistake of limiting it. Those teens who cling to one other person as a sort of life preserver in the storm of adolescence more often than not discover the life preserver to be a stone instead, one which can sink them in the long run.

Scariness is part of everything we call adventure, excitement, thrill. Adolescence is scary at times precisely because it is a challenge—and it is part of the great adventure of creating your life.

You say we can raise parents, but what are parents?

Parent comes from the Latin word *parens,* which means "source." A parent is the biological source of a child. That's as true of bugs as of human beings. Unfortunately, a few people don't take parenthood much further than this.

A good parent accepts a role as both source and co-creator of a new life. A true parent accepts the immense creative task of being guardian and protector of that new person. A true parent has the challenge to be exactly the kind of adult he or she wants this child to become. That's probably the toughest job of all.

As parents, my late wife, Myra, and I saw that the best kind of discipline we could give our eight children was *self*-discipline. If we wanted them to be loving people with a sense of justice and responsibility toward the world, we each had to be that kind of person, too. Basically we were being, in the popular jargon, role models.

Some parents think setting a good example only involves appearances. Naturally, their kids spot their phoniness and recognize that their parents are pretending to uphold certain values that they don't really cherish. Those parents actually are serving as role models for lying.

If I want my kids to be caring, then I really have to care.

If I want my kids to be concerned about other people, then I really have to be concerned about other people. That is what's really tough for parents. Here's where "raising parents" comes in again: my children were a continual challenge to me to live up to my convictions.

What is the difference between a good parent and a bad parent?

In my practice of psychotherapy, and in my wanderings around the world, I have never met a parent who wasn't trying to be the best parent he or she knew how to be.

Some are better parents than their parents were for them. They have improved themselves, possibly after great struggle. Remember, your parents learned to parent from their own mothers and fathers, and perhaps they're doing a pretty good job, given their training. One way you can find out is to get to know your parents not just as parents but as people.

It doesn't help much to focus on whether a parent is "bad" or not but, instead, on ways you can help make things better.

Still, there are traits that good parents seem to have. If you are to become someone who feels worthwhile, who has a healthy self-respect and self-love, you need respect and love from your parents. If they give you time, they tell you you're worthwhile. If they treat you as a person, they tell you you're personable. If they treat you with love, you grow in proper self-love.

Sometimes those things don't happen. But I don't want to discourage you if you feel your parents don't respect or love you. I've never met a parent who wasn't trying.

It's especially crucial in adolescence that you move beyond treating your parents simply as father or mother, because they are more than that. They are persons. They faced the same difficult questions you face now. Ask your dad, "How did you know you were in love with Mom?" Or ask your mom, "How did you feel when you were pregnant with me?"

Ask, "What was your mother like?" "What did your mother tell you about sex?" "What did your father tell you about sex?" "How did you learn about sex?" Those questions may seem frightening to you, but they'll be even more frightening, perhaps, to your parents. And they will open the door to finding out where your parents came from and who they are as persons. They will help you understand how your parents came to be who they are, and that will help you to cope with them and help them grow as parents.

My friend and I were wondering if fathers have periods, too. I think mine does!

Fathers can have cycles. There are fathers who are "day people" and others who are "night people." For example, I gain energy as the day goes on, while some others are winding down.

There are people (including fathers) who have rhythms that seem attuned with longer cycles—days, weeks, months, and even years. Some researchers call these biorhythms and chart them. There are some people whose mood cycles are so severe they need treatment.

It is also possible that at certain times of the month—say, around payday—Dad runs short of funds and starts worrying about bills, about not getting the raise he wants, and maybe even about not reaching the financial goals he set up earlier in life (perhaps when he was an adolescent); so, yes, it could be that every month he gets grumpy.

More important than where your father's moods come from, or whether they are like a woman's menstrual cycles, is how you choose to respond to him at those times. Obviously, when he's in an unhappy mood is not the time to argue or debate an issue with him; try to be as warm, sociable, and noncombative as you can. Because you notice and may even be able to predict your father's mood swings, you can maintain a low profile or perhaps create a positive atmosphere at such times.

Why do parents sometimes seem more irritable than at other times?

In the days just before the menstrual period, some women suffer from what is called Premenstrual Syndrome. The very existence of the premenstrual stress syndrome was questioned a few years ago, but there is no longer any doubt many women experience great distress at those times. Your father's moods may run in cycles as I described in answering the preceding question.

It is also possible your parents have problems you know nothing about. Many youngsters underestimate the economic difficulties of family life. Given housing and food expense and the job insecurities of the modern workplace, your parents could be worried about things they haven't told you but are discussing between themselves.

When you detect negative signals from your parents, apply the principles I just cited. Be as cheerful as you can. Maintain your equilibrium and don't be a source of annoyance at such times.

As an adolescent, you know feelings come and go. What matters is what we do with them.

Sometimes my dad comes home from work and he's really tired and hassled and he'll sit and watch the basketball game on cable TV and guzzle a beer. He doesn't really seem to care about me. Am I doing something wrong?

No. Your father very often will be genuinely fatigued from work and may need a mini-vacation. That may be what you're describing.

But if all he does is sit in front of the TV and have his beer and ignore you and your mother, then you may have a "problem" father. He may have a drinking problem; he may have withdrawn from the family.

If that's the case, the best you can do is be a constructive influence. Invite him to play Monopoly or suggest everyone go to the movies. Try to wake him up. Unfortunately, "couch potatoes" are rather common these days.

Such men are abdicating their roles as fathers and as husbands. If your father is one, show him this response and see what he thinks of it:

Dad, it's one thing to take a mini-vacation and shuck all your responsibilities for a few minutes in front of the tube, but it's another thing to do it continuously. I have counseled families that were completely turned around when the couch potato got up and finally decided it was time to have some fun with his spouse and his family. How about you?

My mom always lays into me after she gets home from work. I'm usually not in a very good mood myself. What can I do?

If you are home first, set the table, take out the garbage, do the dishes, or put some flowers out. Greet your mother warmly in spite of your fatigue. She may be on edge because she had a very hard day and is coming home to more hard work—including cooking dinner and setting the table. Your small gestures of love, your helpfulness, might make her look forward to homecoming.

If you're usually in a bad mood when you come home and do nothing to help, she'll come home expecting you to be grumpy; that makes her more grumpy, and pretty soon you're in a vicious circle.

Somebody has to break the circle. Because you are aware of it, you can improve the emotional climate of your home by making some gestures that will help her. When she comes home, greet her with a smile and say, "Hey, Mom! I washed the dishes." Or you might sit her down and rub her ankles. I guarantee you that will put your relationship ahead by light years. You may also find that your loving gestures are a way of getting yourself in a better mood.

My mom says she's going through menopause. Sometimes she yells at me, and other times she'll cry in the bedroom. It scares me. What is menopause? Is my mom losing her mind?

Menopause in its turmoil can be even worse than adolescence for some women. If puberty is a time the body prepares for parenthood, menopause is the time the woman's body is shutting down those functions. Sharp hormonal changes can bring pain and mood shifts. Your mother may be cheerful one moment in the supermarket and the next crying over the broccoli. She may feel waves of intense heat and sudden nausea; it can be very disconcerting.

Some doctors prescribe estrogen, but it's not a treatment appropriate for everyone. At any rate, any woman who is having a difficult menopause needs a doctor's help and her family's understanding.

Be sympathetic, and be reassured she's not going crazy. It doesn't last forever—although it may seem to your mother that it does.

My mom dresses terribly—tight pink stretch pants and pumps, bright purple lipstick. I hate being seen with her. How can I handle being so ashamed of my mother?

Teenagers dress outrageously, and even wear strange hair styles, but expect their parents to accept it as a "phase." Maybe your mom is going through a phase, too. Show her love and affection, just as you want her to show you.

It often comes as a surprise to adolescents that their

parents are struggling human beings. In your case, your mother may be emulating your growing youthful sexiness even as her own youth leaves her.

Or she may be doing the best she can, with what she has in taste and judgment, to try to appear youthful in a culture that prizes youth. Show your mom some understanding. On her birthday, Mother's Day, and Christmas, buy her some clothes and cosmetics that you think would be flattering.

Why are most parents, teachers, ministers, police, and adults stupid? They're always telling us what to do.

All the people you mention may appear "stupid" to an adolescent from time to time because they lay down rules. Any adolescent sometimes feels that a given rule is "stupid" when it goes against his or her will.

What if these people didn't set down rules? We'd accuse parents of not fulfilling their basic responsibility, which is to set limits for their children so they don't get hurt. Teachers would not be meeting their social obligation and earning their pay unless they set limits and standards for students to live up to.

What would you think if I, as your parent, said to you, "I don't care if you use dope or drink or smoke. I don't care if you drive fast. I don't care how late you stay out. I don't care what kind of grades you get. I don't care what you do with your life. I don't care what you wear. I don't care where you go or who you go with, or what you do!"

What would I be telling you? Of course: I would be saying, "I don't love you. I don't care for you. You are unimportant to me." These adults aren't being stupid; they're trying to set rules to direct and guide you toward choices that will enhance, not hurt, your life.

My parents seem to love making dumb rules.

If you did not find your parents' rules dumb occasionally, there would be something constitutionally wrong with you, and we would have to take you off to a psychologist to find out what.

Your task, if you're growing, is to increase your freedom and your ability to live independently. But as long as you are at home, it is your parents' task to protect you from the many things in the world that can hurt you and to create a harmonious environment for the whole family.

If you and your parents don't have some friction occasionally, then either you're not pushing toward independence as you should or your parents are too permissive.

You can reduce that tension, however. If a rule seems particularly ridiculous, take a look at your parents' motives. Perhaps the rule was right for you a year ago but isn't any more, and your parents have not kept up with you—which isn't uncommon.

Discuss it with them sometime when you are all in a good mood and the specific subject isn't emotionally charged—at a picnic, after church. Simply say, "By the way, about that rule, I'd like to talk with you about it because . . ."

Why are parents always interested in the most unimportant things in your life, never in the important things? Fifty years from now, who'll care whether I got an A or a B in chemistry? What counts is who I am and what my feelings are. Why can't my parents understand that?

That's a very good question. Parents often seem to give importance to the wrong things. Since they can see a grade, and they want you to be working up to your potential, they may look at it and ask, "Are you doing your best?"

Whether you have friends and feel good about yourself

is important too, I agree. The parent who stresses only your grades is missing *you,* and that could be a real loss to him or her. Don't let your parents be losers in this fashion.

Pick a time when grades are not an issue, and tell your mother and father, "You know, I sometimes get the impression that my grades are more important to you than I am."

They may not know you feel this way. Share your feelings with them about this or other issues that are important to you. If they appear uninterested, you might say to them, "I find it difficult to believe that my feelings are unimportant but whether I get an A or a B in chemistry is."

You have to try, from your end of the relationship, to open up honest communication. If you don't try, you may for years carry unfinished business, perhaps resentment, that could have been taken care of right now.

Why is it that when I come home from school or work, my parents don't ask how I've been? Instead, my dad just talks about his job, and my mom nags me.

It sounds as though your parents are preoccupied and may simply assume that you are doing well.

Take the initiative. Pick a time when your father isn't talking about his job, and your mother isn't nagging you. Tell them about something that happened at school today.

I've often had parents approach me after I've talked to students at school and say, "You've done a miraculous thing; my daughter came home today and actually talked to me about something that happened at school!" or "It's amazing! I don't know what you did, but my daughter came home and discussed some of her feelings with us today!" or "My son came home and told us what has going on with him lately!"

All I had done was remind those young people that communication is a two-way street. Some of those who felt their parents weren't listening had not really been opening up. Often parents don't want to invade your privacy, so they talk about themselves; but then you think, "They don't care about what's happening with me."

When's the last time you offered a glimpse into what's been going on with you? If you haven't done that lately, now's the time to do it.

Why do parents always remember the bad things their children do but forget the good?

A lot of people only pay attention to bad things. We do it to ourselves. You might do fifty good things between breakfast and getting to school—tie your shoes right, button your shirt, comb your hair, brush your teeth, put the dishes in the dishwasher or the sink, make your own lunch—then you spill some milk on your clothes and say, "I never do anything right."

Some parents unfortunately take for granted the things you do right and focus on those you do wrong because they think their task is to correct you.

Next time, hear your parents out, and then, with good will, say, "Now that you've listed the things I've done wrong, would you mind telling me some things I do right?"

If that seems too inflammatory, wait until everyone's in a good mood and then say, "You know, I was thinking the other day that I really need to have you tell me some good things about me. I need to feel you notice them."

When my son Michael was seven, he went to his mother one day and said, "Mom, am I a likable person?" Myra replied, "Michael! You're lovable! I love you!" And he said, "Oh, I know you *love* me. I want to know, Am I likable? I mean, do you really *like* me?"

Most of us need that question answered from time to time. Take the risk. Your parents may fail you when you do, but the odds are they won't.

Many parents believe the best way for them to help their children improve is by criticizing what they do wrong. Most teachers mark papers only for errors. All of us do it: we kick ourselves a lot. But kicking ourselves doesn't help us change. It only depresses us. We are both the kicker and the kickee, so we lose energy both ways. No wonder we wind up feeling, What's the use?

Research shows that the best way to improve people is through positive rewards: praise the things people do right. If our parents, our teachers, and we ourselves paid more attention to the things we did right, we would gain strength and energy and wind up doing *more* things right.

So when someone gives you a compliment, don't wave it away. Look at all the answers you got right rather than the three you missed. Ask your parents to say some good things about you from time to time, and do the same for them. Give yourself credit for the good things you've done today.

I never seem able to match up to others. When you say to learn from the good things we do, how can that be?

Too often in adolescence we make ourselves feel bad by thinking we're the only cracked teacup in the set, or by thinking nobody likes us or that we're the wrong size or shape.

You are an absolutely unique human being, and there's nobody else on earth like you; therefore, comparisons with other people don't matter. You bring certain qualities to life and to other people that nobody else can bring. You are irreplaceable. We know that from genetics. We know that from theology and philosophy. No two of us are ever alike.

That being so, you have to begin looking at your unique beauty, talents, and contributions to the world.

If you see just that you have a crooked nose or that your test scores are too low, or that you make mistakes in life, you deplete yourself. You lower your morale, and then, because you have low self-esteem, you may end up wondering why grades matter. You may end up using drugs or alcohol, or being promiscuous, because you don't think you're worth saving. All these further damage your self-esteem, so you look for further escape. You could destroy yourself.

By focusing on the positive, you *increase* your self-esteem. You gain more energy, and then you can do more good things; pretty soon both you and other people approve of you even more. It's an upward spiral.

People who do not look like movie stars, who have no great physical attributes, or even great intellectual gifts, by using the gifts they do have can be successful both academically and socially.

Your attractiveness has nothing to do with a nose job; the person who is attractive is the person who radiates positive energy. How do you get positive energy? By being positive about yourself and taking a positive attitude toward other people.

Why do parents always interpret what their teenagers say to mean something horrible?

If your parents seem to jump to bad conclusions, they're probably doing so out of fear.

This is a fearful time to be the parent of an adolescent. Thousands of pre-teen and teenaged boys and girls simply disappear each year. The most horrible things happen to them. In addition, hundreds of thousands of young people each year get venereal disease, sometimes with lifelong consequences, including sterility for girls. A million girls get pregnant each year with the aid of a million underage boys. There are uncountable murders and rapes and assaults of other sorts. Alcoholism and drug addiction among young people are epidemic.

Parents read these terrible facts in the newspaper and become worried. Because they do not want these things to happen to you, they tend to focus on them to try to keep them away from you.

So, the next time your parents misinterpret something you say in some awful way, listen very patiently and try to hear the fear that is behind their words. Don't become defensive. You might even want to say, "I am hearing that you are afraid of . . .," and, "Are you afraid of that with regard to me?"

Pursue the matter a bit. It could be that your parents don't know how to express their fear. You may have to help them express it. The parent who screams at you when you come home an hour and a half after curfew was just moments before sweating with fear that something dreadful had happened to you. Instead of "Oh! I'm so glad you're home! I was scared something terrible had happened to you!" you hear "Where in the hell have you been?"

Generally, angry outbursts cover up feelings of fear or feelings of inadequacy.

Another point: Adolescents tend to say "always," "never," "everything," "everybody." But when you think your parents "always" do something, remember that "always" is a pretty strong word. One sign of maturity is realizing that very few people "always" and very few people "never." Knowing that will help you understand, and therefore raise, your parents more successfully.

I'm the youngest in a large family, and I think my parents are tired of being parents. Almost anything I do is okay with them as long as I don't crack up the car or get in trouble. I really like the freedom, but it bothers me they often don't seem to have the time or energy for me. What about this?

Many teenagers would envy you, but what you are saying is that you don't feel loved.

Your parents might really be tired, or they may have simply eased up on setting limits as their family grew. Although I did set limits for my eighth child, the limits were much broader than those I set for my first child. I've grown more aware that I cannot really protect my children from everything. I've matured a great deal as a parent.

But that doesn't mean I don't care. Your parents may have learned to relax the reins a bit. They trust you a great deal and it may be that scares you.

Say to your mother or your father, "You know, sometimes I get scared with all this responsibility," or "I'd like to know what you think about . . ."

Adolescence and puberty is a scary time; one of the ways you can feel secure is by making sure you have some boundaries so you don't hurt yourself. You find security in those boundaries, even though you push against them.

One of the paradoxes of adolescence is that even as we're grabbing for freedom, freedom scares us. When nobody accepts responsibility we have to be responsible for ourselves.

If your parents really have abdicated their responsibilities, recognize your fear as realistic, look to your older sisters and brothers for guidance occasionally, and continue to show yourself responsible in spite of your fear.

You're just growing up faster that way.

If I have a real problem, should I talk to the other kids in my family? Or would my parents get mad about that?

One of the great advantages of having older brothers and sisters is that they become part of your support group for life. They care about you and can give you insight and help. First, though, try to talk to your parents as your major source of insight.

My parents have to have a say in everything I do: whether I take geometry or algebra two years from now, whether I go out for soccer or football, whether I wear a belt with my jeans, whether I eat popcorn or candy at the movies. I get so angry sometimes I want to run away, but then they'd probably tell me where, how, and when to run. What's going on with them?

Your parents mean well but are oversupervising. They are not allowing you the latitude that's necessary for someone your age. You might do well to remind them of the fourth commandment—not the first part, but the second part, which many parents tend to forget: The first part, as quoted by St. Paul, is, "Children, honor your father and your mother." The second part is, "And parents, do not rouse your children to resentment."

One way of rousing children's resentment is by over-supervising them. Your parents' idea that "I know best for you in every detail" limits your freedom and is an insult to your intelligence.

We come to a key word again: *talk.* Talk to your parents about this. If you don't feel you can talk to them in person, sit down and write a letter in which you state as clearly as you know how exactly what you resent. Couch your letter in love (they do love you—they are just expressing their love in an overprotective fashion). Let them know they are rousing your resentment. And let them know you love them and you're not going to let them down, but you need freedom to make some decisions about your own life.

If they keep this up, they may make it very difficult for you to cut the umbilical cord without rebelling totally. Many parents have come to me complaining about their youngsters ignoring them and rebelling against them—and often we discover these parents created their own plight by overcoercive and overcontrolling behavior.

Perhaps you should show them this answer. You still want their counsel and advice, and you prize their greater wisdom, because of their greater knowledge of the world, but at the same time you need to make some decisions for yourself.

Some parents oversupervise for other reasons. A father who didn't make varsity may want his son to be a varsity star to make up for it. A mother who didn't make cheerleader may want her daughter to be a cheerleader so she can enjoy it vicariously. These parents have confused themselves about the place of their own egos. If your parents are like that, then you will have to cut the umbilical cord from your end.

For other parents, a growing child is evidence they themselves are older. If their major role has been mother or father, they may find it hard to let go. They keep trying, even when it's no longer appropriate, to make all the decisions. If that is true of your parents, they are refusing to recognize you're growing older (because that means recognizing that they are growing older too). They're simply going to have to let go and let you have more freedom. Time is on your side in this.

One way of cutting the cord is to choose a college in another city or state.

What if they get mad at me for writing them a letter like the one you mentioned?

Say in the letter, "You may be angry with me for telling you how I feel, but I have done it out of love and out of a desire to have a better understanding between us." Their anger will be rooted in fear: the fear that they are losing you, and losing control of you.

As I noted earlier, parents who set no limits create large problems for their children. But overcontrolling parents create problems just as large.

Parents who set no limits and can't maintain consistent authority often produce children who feel no sense of security in the world. Such children are the ones who go into cults, gangs, and totalitarian organizations in search of the security they lack. Or they may simply lead chaotic and undisciplined lives.

Parents who drastically overcontrol their kids produce children who lead lives of rebellion against all authority. Such children grow up unable to give the proper respect to authorities such as their boss at work, the police, the state, moral codes. The result is, again, chaotic lives.

It's difficult for parents to strike that balance, and that's where you have to help. Your parents must gradually relinquish control and authority, and you must gradually take on more responsibility. Family life is a collaboration. Sometimes your parents will be out of step; sometimes you will be. Both of you have to work to bring things back into harmony. Above all, don't give up trying to talk to your parents.

Why can't parents believe kids have problems just as they themselves do?

You seem to be saying you feel you have problems and your parents haven't listened to you. Perhaps your parents think yours are childish problems, but that is no reason for them to disregard those problems. Your problems are very real to you. Your parents should be made aware of them.

Possibly you need to approach your parents differently. If you hide in your room, they probably don't know what your problems are.

As a psychotherapist, I'd insist on sitting down with you. If you've been "acting out" your feelings—acting sullen and withdrawn—you probably expect your parents to know how you're feeling. But they aren't mind readers. Is it so difficult to walk up to one of your parents and say, "Can I have five minutes of your time?" or "I need to tell you what's bugging me"?

Most parents will say "Sure!" If you haven't tried that approach, don't say they don't know you have problems.

As a parent, I've taken the initiative from time to time with my children: "I need to hear what's going on with you." If your parents don't do this, you may have to take that initiative yourself.

How do you deal with a mother who admits she playacts all her feelings when she doesn't feel right? You never know how she really feels.

I'm assuming you mean that she does things like hiding her anger behind a mask of niceness, or her sadness behind a facade of cheerfulness.

If your mother admitted that to you, you might want to recommend she seek therapy. She's behaving inauthentically. On the other hand, her honesty about this is a good sign. She dropped her mask long enough to disclose that about herself.

When your mother playacts a feeling, don't accept it at face value. Instead, ask, "What are you really feeling right now?" or "Could you put that into other words?" or "What would you like me to do in response to that?"

Answering these questions would make your mother clarify things for herself as well as you. It's a direct method to help her analyze herself. Now that she's given you the clue, tell her, "Well, you're behaving this way, but I'm not sure what it means. Would you mind telling me?" You could help her grow that way.

But she might need therapy, and you might suggest it. Don't say, "Hey, Mom, you need to see a psychologist!" Instead, tell her you want to go in with her to improve mother-child communication, which is, of course, the truth. It would help her to learn why she playacts, and it would surely improve your relationship with her.

Why does a father's pride make him defend his position no matter what —instead of accepting the truth or accepting new knowledge a teenager might have to offer?

It's not only your father who does that. Lots of people have weak egos; just because a man fathers children doesn't mean he has a strong ego. A man with a weak ego is constantly on the defensive, feeling he must always be right. He has to prove you're wrong in order to give himself a sense of strength. Perhaps this is true of your father.

But if he pulverizes you, what has he proved? He's got a "loser" for a kid. He needs to learn you can totally disagree with one another and still be very close friends. He can be a Republican and you a Democrat, and you can argue politics and be great friends. In other words, agreement is not where it's at.

There was a time fathers did have to be right. If your father grew up on a farm, for example, his father had to be right. He made the decision when to plant the crops and when to harvest. He decided what was to be done during the day. He had enormous authority. Indeed, the entire economic life of the family depended on him. The family was isolated, and someone had to make those decisions. The father was the most experienced farmer in the family; therefore, when a father on a farm made a decision it was not questioned. Your father may have learned how to be a parent from such a father. But that sort of parental authority no longer applies in our contemporary urban world.

Unfortunately, people who always have to be right can never learn anything. They're so busy defending themselves that they don't listen to other people.

You might seek help on how to cope with your father, whom I would call a "toxic person." In other words, he's someone who tends to poison the wellspring of others' good feelings. You don't want that to happen to you. Accept him as he is. Don't debate him. You know you're not going to have intelligent discourse, because he'll turn it into a contest. Talk to your mother, or talk to your aunt or uncle, or someone else. You can seek to understand your father, even if he doesn't seek to understand you. And, unless he changes his ways, part of that understanding is that there is no point trying to tell him anything.

I still do love him. Should I give in to whatever he's saying, no matter what I really think?

Always remember your relationship with your father (or anyone else in your family) is more important than whatever topic you're discussing. The topic can be very important, but it's less important than your relationship.

Avoid arguments. Try to have discussions, dialogue, or conversations. If you don't worry about winning or losing, you'll help put your relationship with your father on a different footing. And if you care to risk it, you might want to make an observation about the process, and say, "You know, I'd like to discuss something with you and I don't want to bring it into who's right and who's wrong, I just want to have your opinion on this and maybe your insight into this and it's not a matter of right or wrong." And if he starts into right or wrong, say, "I really don't want to talk about right or wrong in this one, I just want talk about it."

My father will bait me by saying negative things about things he knows I care about. He says he has to "reeducate" me because I'm too liberal. What should I do?

Ignore it. Just because he presses button *A* doesn't mean you have to give response *B*. Refuse inside yourself to get involved in a losing debate. Keep your own counsel. He's doing it in order to get an issue raised that he wants to sound off on. Your question indicates that he believes education to be a one way street, so he's not really going to listen to you except to combat what you say.

Since you know the outcome, be a noncombatant and sit on the sidelines. You can say, "That's interesting. Is there some reason you brought that up?" or "You know I disagree with you, so why don't we just not discuss it." Use your ingenuity to respond in a way that leaves you free to do something else. Turn the conversation by saying, "Did I tell you about the basketball game this afternoon?" or "Did I tell you about what happened in chemistry class this morning?"

Many people allow others to manipulate them with in-

flammatory statements. If, however, you are no longer pre-
dictable in your responses, they quit pressing those buttons.

Why don't parents understand the problems of the world today?

I think you're really saying your parents don't understand *you.* How well they understand you depends on how
much you reveal to them about what's going on in the world
of young people.

Reveal your ideas, but do it in a nonthreatening fashion.
Don't sound as if you believe that "all kids are right, and all
parents are wrong." That's a natural tendency of young
people. It may help if you realize your parents were once
kids themselves. Say, "Did you feel that way when you
were young?"

You'll probably find your parents at some point in their
own adolescence felt all adults were wrong, and didn't understand the world, and that kids were the only ones with
a handle on truth. As you mature you'll discover that few
of the issues of the world are easily resolvable. There are
large gray areas and areas where two points of view can both
be entertained with equal validity. It's a sign of maturity to
be able to entertain a diversity of opinions and see things
from other points of view.

Can an immature parent cause a child to grow up faster?

Yes, there's no doubt about it. If a parent is behaving in
a childish way or abdicating responsibility (which is immature, because maturity means accepting responsibility),
then the child very often takes over and becomes a parent.
Somebody has to. Many of my clients began to parent at
an early age because their parents were drinking, taking
drugs, or simply not accepting normal parental respon-

sibilities. One man, because his father was an alcoholic, had to be a parent to all the younger children. Another, a woman, as a girl had to take responsibility for the other children because her single mother abdicated parental duties and drank too much.

The trouble is, such kids lose out on the freedom to be children, on the freedom to be irresponsible at an age when responsibilities are supposed to be carried by parents. They have to parent themselves, and that's an enormous responsibility.

Why do parents think they should raise you the way they were raised? I've heard them gripe about their own parents.

They probably don't think about it at all. Unless we rationally decide to do it differently than our parents did, we will unconsciously raise our kids the way we were raised. Many abusive parents, for example, were themselves abused children. In other words, their role models weren't very good. Because they failed to reflect on that sufficiently and consciously decide to behave differently, they act just as their parents did.

In your case, you're getting mixed messages. Your parents' behavior is like their parents', but consciously they reject part of it. This gives you an opening. Ask your parents —again, in a nonthreatening way—"What didn't you like about the way you were brought up?" The answer may increase understanding for both you and your parents.

Why does my mom get mad when I try to brush her hair, even though I'm trying to make her look as young as possible?

I would not seek to brush anyone's hair without that person's permission. And you're implying your mother looks old; I'm not surprised she resents that. Perhaps you should find another means of showing your affection.

Why do parents always seem to forget how they felt when they were adolescents?

Perhaps because for most people puberty and adolescence were a nightmare. The hard questions, the ups and downs emotionally, may have been so painful your parents repressed their memories of it.

I'm a college student. For various reasons my childhood was less than ideal. How can I leave some of the pain behind me when I go on to have my own family?

One of the great glories of having children (when you're a mature adult) is that they provide a marvelous opportunity to redo your own childhood.

If you didn't ride carousels as a child, then as a parent you can ride carousels with your children and let the child in you play. If, like me, you didn't have anybody read you bedtime stories, you can read your kids all kinds of stories —complete with gestures and great drama. And as your children move into adolescence, you can go back and, in a sense, reevaluate your own adolescence and make it less painful.

A warning, though: The sooner you rush into marriage, the less chance your marriage and new family will have. Research shows that up to the age of twenty-five, every year you wait cuts the likelihood of divorce. And though parenthood is rewarding, it is also, as I've pointed out, an enormous responsibility. Your patience, your sense of humor, your capacity for understanding and loving and caring will be tested daily.

How are teenagers supposed to deal with parents who always hark back to what they had or were able to do when it comes to us asking for something?

"When I was your age . . ." Is that what your parents say? They were never your age. Yours is a different family, different climate, different age from theirs when they grew up. They had different parents. It's possible their own mothers and fathers came from a different culture. My father was born in 1880 before the airplane, the light bulb, the automobile changed the way we live. When I was born, it was a whole different world. He couldn't say, "When I was your age."

I was born before the A-bomb, jets, Hitler. My children were born after all these things. I saw the A-bomb as a relief; it meant the war would end. My kids see a nuclear world teetering on the brink of destruction. It's a different world.

When you hear, "When I was your age," step back and ask, "Yes, but how does that apply to me at this moment?" "I can appreciate that that's what you went through, but are you telling me I'm supposed to go through the same thing?" In other words, try to clarify why your parents are thinking back at that particular moment.

Thank them for sharing their history. And then say, "But that still leaves us with the question of this issue."

It's possible they think you're not grateful enough. I know of a father, newly rich, who bought his son a car. When the son said, "Thanks, Dad," and drove off, Dad grumbled, "He's not really grateful enough!" Dad was really saying, "In the middle of the depression I would have been enormously grateful if someone had given me a car."

He was commenting on himself rather than his son.

Step back from those scenes and puzzle out what it is

your parents are trying to say. Are they saying you should express more appreciation? Then express more appreciation. Do they want you to know not everything comes easy in life? Puzzle it out.

Did parents have problems with schoolwork when they were young?

Are parents human? Of course they had problems with schoolwork. Unfortunately, some parents pretend they always did their homework delightedly and got straight A's; walked to school through blinding snowstorms straight uphill (both coming and going), without lunch; and when they got home did all the chores on the farm as well as cleaned the whole house.

Somehow they think this idealization of their own childhood will be an inspiration for their children instead of a put-down.

Ask your parents if they have their old report cards around anywhere. Though they mean well when they tell these stories, parents tend to be a bit selective when contrasting their own work to what they might see as poor academic performance on your part.

Every time I want to do something, like going on a chaperoned camping trip or to a party where someone (not me) might use drugs, or like getting a job after school that means I'm downtown some nights, my parents have endless discussions without ever deciding anything. They can't seem to make up their minds. So sometimes I just go ahead and do whatever it is, and that makes them mad. Why is it so hard for them to decide?

They don't want to make the wrong decision. One way for them to avoid making a wrong decision is not to make one at all. Then when you make the decision, they can jump on you. They're probably secretly relieved you decided for them.

That's apparently one of the rules in your family: Your parents absolve themselves of responsibility, and they blame you if things go wrong.

This is a good example of how families keep unwritten rules. Some families have a rule that says, "Daddy is a drunk, but only Mommy gets to say that" or "The girls always do the dishes unless they have something really important to do, and then the boys will be asked to do them."

When you put all the rules together, you get what amounts to your family culture, which is unique.

The problem is that sometimes your family culture was formed ten or more years ago, and it still remains, even though all kinds of changes have occurred in your parents' lives as well as in yours. Some of those rules no longer make sense.

You can play the family game according to that rule, or you can instead decide to discuss the rule. Some nice afternoon on a family picnic, you can say to your parents, "Are you aware that when I want a decision about something, you two talk it over and over and over until I have to make the decision myself and then you criticize my decision? Clay Barbeau says that that's one of our family rules and that it's a way of avoiding responsibility."

As they set boundaries, parents must recognize they have a maturing child. Some parents aren't willing to do that. Or perhaps, as with your parents, they must recognize their own responsibility. Some parents aren't willing to do that. This arena is a challenge and stressful for both sides. Bringing up an adolescent can be an adventure—or an awful time —for parents. It can be "distressing" or "eustressing." It's stressful either way. *Distress* means "bad" stress. *Eustress* means "good" stress. In most things, it is our attitude that determines whether stress is a source of pain or an adventure.

If parents are safety nets for children, then in some ways children are safety nets for parents. Children give parents a sense of control over an uncontrollable world, and some parents don't let go of that easily.

My mom and I have a very close relationship. I'm worried about her reaction to my going off to college. Once, I wanted to go to boarding school, and she reacted very badly. Why? Is there anything I can do to ease the situation?

Perhaps. A woman came to me because her daughter had gone away to college. The daughter was ecstatic about going to college, but the mother cried for a week—literally sobbed for a week. She had lost her parental role.

The wise parent, with the aid of the wise young person, must move from a parent-child relationship to a friend-friend one. Your parents should become, before you are thirty years old, your best friends, second only to your spouse. That's the goal: the equal status of intimates.

Who knows you more intimately than your parents—except perhaps your spouse? How much more intimate can someone get than to change your diapers? Breast-feed you? Watch you grow? Watch you learn to walk? Help you learn to talk?

But the process of disengaging from a parent-child relationship and building an adult-adult one can mean traumatic changes for parents. Your growing up signals your independence from your mother, and she has invested a large chunk of her emotional life in being "your mother."

Reassure her in every way you can that you love her dearly, and that you think it's wonderful that you're moving on into this new adult-adult relationship. And that just because you don't need her parenting anymore does not mean you don't need her as your best friend in the world.

Let her know that you're cutting the umbilical cord, but she can stand on her own two feet. That she's capable of being independent of you. These are the messages you must get across.

Earlier I mentioned the students I spoke to in Seattle. One by one they described how "My father can hardly stand it that I've gone away from home to college; my mother is heartbroken and she weeps and cries all the time over the phone."

After our group talk, the consensus these young adults reached was that the more they required independence, the more their parents protested, and thus, the more necessary it was they constantly reassure their parents that they still loved them.

Your growth—your going away to college—leaves a new space your parents can fill with new independence, new freedom, new delight in life. They're free of the responsibility of setting limits, of confrontation, of raising an adolescent.

It may seem ironic that however much some parents complain about parenting an adolescent, many still prefer it. Some are terrified of confronting their husband or wife alone —without the buffer of their children—for the rest of their lives! They can't constantly argue about the children anymore. They're going to have to relate to one another and to the world in a new fashion. And that scares some of them.

So it's crucial for you to understand now that parents need all the reassurance you can give them. You have to encourage—put courage into—them. Tell them they really can be independent of you and still survive.

2

War and Peace

2

Is it a law of nature that parents and teenagers can't agree on anything?

Not necessarily. At school probably three or four of your classmates would tell you they're best friends with their fathers or mothers, and it would be true.

But they're a distinct minority. Most of us have had problems communicating with our parents. That's why I'm writing this book, to help you and your parents communicate better.

Of course, some conflict is inevitable. It's in the nature of things. If you're a healthy adolescent, you're asserting your independence with ever increasing energy. If your parents are healthy, they're trying to keep you from being killed (or killing your future). It's a dangerous world for teenagers: every hour, a young person is killed in an auto crash related to drinking; an estimated twelve thousand teenagers commit suicide each year; a million girls a year get pregnant; three million kids today are alcoholics; sexually transmitted diseases are widespread.

Your parents are protecting you by setting limits, trying their best to make them reasonable limits. You keep bumping into the limits. There's bound to be conflict.

Not all conflict is bad. Take a handful of old stones, throw them in a rock tumbler and turn the machine on. Listen to those rough old stones rubbing against one another. There's lots of friction in there. But before too long, when you take out the stones, they've become polished and beautiful.

In the same way, healthy conflict can enhance you and your parents. Any family with growing youngsters and growing parents is going to have friction, but it's a friction that helps us all grow. The friction of family life is meant to polish us up.

Good family communication will take away most of the unnecessary friction and self-created pain, leaving a healthy pinch to grow on.

Why does my mother always nag when she first sees me?

Perhaps your mother is unhappy or insecure. Perhaps she had a nagging mother herself, and so thinks mothering means nagging.

It's also possible that what you call nagging she thinks is telling you that she had to pick up your clothes and do other things you were supposed to take care of. She may have been storing up a laundry list of complaints during her day. When people remind us of things we haven't done and feel guilty about not having done, we call that "nagging."

However, it's not so important why she nags you as how you choose to respond to it.

Listen to her. What is she really trying to say?

If her complaints are legitimate, then the next day try to avoid giving her cause for those complaints.

If she still nags you, in spite of your efforts, it's probably time to talk to her.

Tell her, "Mom, could we work out a more pleasant welcome home?"

Tell her, "Are you aware that whenever I come home, you start by saying (whatever it is) and I find that very depressing, I find it a downer. Aren't you glad to see me?"

And here's probably the very best thing you can do: When you first come home, and she runs through her list of complaints, let it fly right past you. Then go up to her and say, "I love you, Mom, and it's good to be home."

If you follow these suggestions, I think your mother will stop nagging you.

Why do we have to do what our parents tell us to do and they never do what we tell them to do?

Your parents have legal, moral, and ethical responsibility for your welfare. Until you are eighteen, in most states, your parents are responsible for you. Therefore, given the responsibility, they also have the authority to make rules for you. It doesn't apply in the other direction.

However, authority should always commend itself in love, and I hope your parents, in exercising their authority, are doing it lovingly.

Soon enough you will be paying your own bills—not just financially, but psychologically and emotionally, too. When you're totally independent of your parents, you will have authority over your own life.

In the meantime, in a well-functioning family, a maturing young person should be given increasing authority over his or her actions and decisions and even allowed to make more and more of his or her own mistakes.

What about rules like when I can watch TV or what show I can watch?

Television is of enormous importance in our culture. Your parents have to make sure watching TV doesn't interfere with your academic performance or keep you from your social and athletic activities.

If you're average, you will, by the time you graduate

from high school, have had eleven thousand hours of class-room work and seen over twenty thousand hours of television. For each hour of television you will have seen, on average, one murder. The daily diet of TV is batterings, rapes, arsons, car thefts, burglaries, or situations involving pimps, prostitutes, or drugs. And 92 percent, by some estimates, of all the sexual activity on television is immoral or illegal, that is it is rape, adultery, prostitution or takes place outside of the context of marriage. The latest studies of the effect of violence in TV and films—especially violence against women—indicate that watching such shows often increases this kind of behavior in the viewers.*

So, responsible parenting means exercising some degree of control, depending on your age, over the television set.

My parents tell me I have to leave when they're on the phone, but they don't leave when I'm on the phone.

Your parents are setting a double standard, and that's unfortunate. You have as much right to privacy as your parents do.

Raise the issue, but don't do it in an argumentative way. Simply say, "It hurts my feelings that you don't trust me to talk to my friends on the phone privately. You want privacy on the phone, which is right, so why can't I have it too?"

As a parent, I don't eavesdrop on my kids' phone calls, or go foraging in their rooms, and I expect the same courtesy from them. The best way parents teach their kids about privacy is by giving them privacy.

Your complaint is just.

---

*Michael Rothenberg, M.D., "Sexual Effects of Movie and TV Violence," *Medical Aspects of Human Sexuality,* July 1986.

If your parents smoke, should they tell you not to smoke and look through your belongings for cigarettes?

No. Your mother and father should try to be the kind of people they want you to be. What they do speaks more profoundly than what they say.

I don't imagine they want you to learn to be the kind of person who reads other people's mail or goes through their belongings. Those are invasions of privacy.

I advise that you try not to follow your parents' bad examples, however, including smoking. Invading privacy is bad enough, but smoking adds injury to insult.

It is an irony of our time that while many men and boys are giving cigarettes up girls are actually increasing their smoking.

Smoking is not only injurious to your health, it increases the likelihood of health problems for a woman's unborn children.

One recent study suggests smoking is addictive. Your parents may be addicts. Perhaps you can help them stop— but, of course, you'd have to stop, too.

Use some of the communications techniques I discuss elsewhere in this book to sit down with your parents and ask them to respect your privacy and personhood.

What do you do when your mom and dad yell at you for something, and then they do it themselves?

Talk to them about it.

What your parents are doing is called projecting. That means they're yelling at you for something they don't like in themselves. It's not unusual. "Projection" may be part of the problem with smoking parents who try to stop their kids, too.

Choose a time and place when the issue is not charged with emotion, when your parents aren't criticizing you, and you're not shouting, "But you do it!" Say, "You know, I was just wondering, the other day you both got angry at me because (whatever it was), and it's something you both do, could you explain that?"

If they get angry, drop the subject; you're not going to win. But at least you know that they are projecting onto you their anger at themselves. They care about you and don't want to see you do things they don't like in themselves.

Mom once told me she was twenty when she had to leave college because she was pregnant and get married; now all she does is suspect me of having sex whenever I'm with my boyfriend and yells at me about it.

Your mom knows from firsthand experience what might happen, and it terrifies her. That's why she attacks you and criticizes you. Yelling—attack language—is spelled *f-e-a-r*.

Try this approach: "Mom, I know you get scared when I go out, because of your own experience, but I'm not letting that happen to me. I think you can trust me."

For the first few times, she'll probably argue the point a bit. But if you respond with understanding, not anger, her fears will fade more and more.

And when her fears fade, so will her yelling.

What should a kid do if his dad yells at him for no reason when he's upset about something else?

If you can, remain calm and let him blow off his anger. Then say, "I love you, Dad. I don't think I did anything wrong, but I'm sorry you're upset about something."

Your father is doing what is called displacing. That means when he's angry about something or someone else, he puts her anger in the wrong place—in this case, on you.

It's important that you remember he's not really mad at you. If you can respond by expressing your love for him at times like that, he may stop.

What should a child who is being abused do?

If you are being physically abused or sexually molested, report it immediately to a counselor at school or your doctor or a teacher you trust. Tell a responsible adult immediately. There is a national child abuse hot line you can call toll-free: 1–800–4–A–CHILD.

Because you're embarrassed, because you love your family, or because you have been threatened and are afraid, you may think you should keep it a secret. But that won't help you, and it won't help the person who is abusing you. You must tell someone in authority. Once you tell someone, you can start healing yourself and your family.

How do you cope with a parent who has an extreme illness and blames it on you?

First, don't believe it. You cannot have caused your parent's disease.

Second, talk immediately to your parent's doctor. It is important the doctor know that the illness is causing a mental problem (or the medical treatment is affecting your parent's mind). The doctor may be able to help in this situation.

Third, talk to another adult. Talk to your other parent, to a counselor at school, to your clergyman, or to a teacher about this. You must seek help so you can cope with the guilt your parent is trying to put on you, which you don't deserve. If you can, see someone on a weekly basis for a while.

If you make the mistake of accepting blame for your parent's sickness, you may suffer for a lifetime. That was true of a man whose wife brought him into my office for help. He was deeply depressed and didn't know why.

Eventually, I discovered his mother used to kid him good-naturedly by saying, "You'll be the death of me yet!"

When he was twelve years old, he came home from school one day, walked into the house, and found his mother lying dead on the kitchen floor. She'd had a heart attack.

For more than twenty-five years he privately carried this nasty, guilty secret. He actually thought he had killed his mother.

If mere kidding can cause that kind of guilt, a situation like yours could do even worse damage. That's why you should seek counseling immediately—and tell your parent's doctor.

Is it common for children to be jealous of their parents?

No. If you are, you might want to look at what it is you're jealous of. Is it their maturity? Good looks? Intelligence? If so, you you can be proud of being their child. Sometimes it all depends on how you choose to view it.

It's more common for a parent to be jealous of a daughter's youth or a son's good looks or their childrens' just-awakening sense of personhood and sexuality.

Every time I'm seen talking with a boy, all I get from my mother is, "So, now you've got eyes for John?" or "I saw you and John together; what were you doing?" I associate with nice boys, so there seems to be no reason for this. It's getting to the point where I can't tell her anything.

Your mother is expressing her fear when she implies your friendships with boys might be sexual. Parents very often fear their children becoming sexually involved, because sexual activity among young people so often leads to pregnancy, disease, lowered self-esteem, school dropouts, a whole list of problems.

It would be much healthier in our society if boys and girls could be friends without parents and other people leaping to the conclusion that they are becoming sexually involved.

It would also be healthier if young people could be friends with members of the opposite sex without settling down with one boyfriend or girlfriend. By meeting and becoming friends with many people we become comfortable with them, and we're more likely to make good, mature marriage decisions later on.

Your mother may simply be trying to find out what kind of relationship you have with John. What you want to do is allay her fears. So you can say, "It's okay, Mom, he's a nice boy. He's just another friend of mine."

A "global response" is the best answer to some of her questions. You say, "Oh, John's a very nice boy. You'd like him."

What did you talk about? "Oh, just the usual things."

It is very healthy for you to have a number of friends who are boys, and it's unfortunate that your mother seems to imply they all have to be romantic or sexual relationships. But, remember, she may have been raised similarly by her parents. You might want to ask her about that.

Why is there so much tension when I ask permission to go out with someone of the opposite sex? Isn't there enough trust between me and my parents?

Because the fear of what might happen looms large in parents' minds. Parents are under great stress because of the trouble so many kids get into today.

Let them know you don't intend to be one of those

statistics, that they can trust you, that they've done a good job of raising you and giving you good values.

You can say, "I behave responsibly on these dates. You raised me correctly, and I think you can trust me."

Unfortunately, parents with their fear, distrust, and accusations of wrongdoing sometimes cause kids to say, "The hell with it. If you're accusing me anyway, why not just go ahead and do it?" Above all, don't let that happen to you. It would be self-destructive.

How do you handle a father who can't forgive and forget?

A father who uses your mistakes as a weapon against you needs help. Give him a copy of *Love Is Letting Go of Fear,* by Gerald Jampolsky. It has a section on forgiveness.

You may not be able to change your father, but you can at least not allow *his* problem to fester inside *you.*

When he brings up something from the past, and you really have outgrown it, say: "Is there a particular reason that you're bringing it up now?" That may prompt him to look at his motives.

Or you can say, "What do you want me to say to that?" Then, perhaps, he will examine what it is he's after.

Someone who refuses to forgive and forget is trying to control you through guilt. All of us, including your father, need forgiveness—always. Forgiveness flows out of understanding that we all need to be forgiven from time to time for the dumb things we've done.

How do you make your mom and dad understand that times have changed since they were kids and we do things differently now?

Your parents know very well that times have changed— and that's what scares them.

When I was in high school, for example, the only boys who were on drugs or marijuana were members of a youth gang, most of whom ended up in jail as time went on. Kids who had any self-respect did not take drugs.

Today drugs are used by kids in grade school. Violence, suicide, alcoholism, and sex are far more prevalent among young people now than they were when your parents were kids. Your parents know that.

Reassure your parents that although times have changed, your standards are solid. Tell them you are coping with today's world, even though they may be a bit bewildered and scared of it. If they could learn to see the world from your point of view, it might help them immensely.

Don't try to do this by arguing, but rather by talking with them. Ask them about their high school days, and listen to their answers. Offer your observations on how things are different now—not better or worse, but different. Their fears are about you. Reassure them—by talking and by living responsibly.

What do you do when your parents accuse you of doing something you didn't do, and they really think you did it?

Don't argue the point too much. Try to let go of your anger and dismay, and see if you can figure out how they got the idea you've done something you haven't. They must have, in their own minds, some reasons. If the reasons are irrational, you won't be able to change their minds. Some people do have low expectations of their children, or even "project" their own inclinations onto their children.

I suggest you talk to your school counselor or a teacher you trust about the specifics of any particular problem.

I'm a young adult (20), and I just don't trust my mother anymore. It's a long story—she hasn't been honest with me; she's interfered in my life; and she just has never accepted me. But it bothers me that my own mother and I really don't even like each other. Is this unusual?

Yes, it's relatively unusual. If it's true that your mother has never accepted you—then she is suffering from a deep inner problem and should be in therapy. I would suggest that you have some sessions together to work out the anger and other issues in your relationship.

Also, you do well to try to maintain a positive feeling for your mother. You're responsible only for your end of the relationship. Show affection and love in whatever ways are open to you—a card on Mother's Day, for example—and try not to let her feelings influence you too much.

If you're male, it's possible that you remind her of her father, her husband, or some other man in her life that she dislikes or distrusts; if you're female, you may remind her of her mother or sister. She may have transferred feelings about them onto you, because you're a nearer target.

The best way she can clear that up from her end is through therapy.

Until that time, there's no need for you to respond to her dislike for you by disliking her.

If you nurture a dislike for her, you'll be carrying it around for a long time. Disliking your mother won't help you, and it certainly won't help her. Remember, you're responsible for how you feel toward her. You simply may have to accept her as she is. It's always best to forgive and to continue to love despite how the other person acts toward us.

If you are still living at home, it may be a good idea to move out. A few individual sessions with a therapist may help you understand that your mother's problem must not be allowed to ruin your life.

If parents really love us, why do they punish us?

If your parents love you, they will, indeed, discipline you.

Disciplining means your parents sit down with you and try to discern what happened. What were you hoping to accomplish when you splashed paint on the school pillar? How did you dent the family car? What were you thinking when you broke curfew twice in a row?

Then it means discussing how to right the wrong. If you have dented the car, for example, perhaps you will be responsible for doing the insurance paperwork, getting repair bids, and paying the deductible.

Particularly with teenagers, discipline means stressing that you are responsible for your actions. If you break a rule, just as when you dent the car, you are responsible for doing what is necessary to restore the balance, the trust that was broken.

That's discipline.

Punishment, on the other hand, smacks of revenge. Usually the only thing punishment accomplishes is to prove that somebody else is stronger than you are. Punishment is what we base our prison system on; considering that somewhere between 80 and 90 percent of inmates who get out of prison soon return, punishment obviously doesn't work.

If your parents are disciplining you, the reason is that they love you and are helping you grow up.

Is grounding fair after you've broken curfew or gotten a speeding ticket?

Yes. The idea is to prove to you that, as a young, maturing human being, you are accountable for your actions. If you've done something wrong, you have to right it the best you can, or at least pay the penalty.

You can't right the wrong for breaking curfew or for speeding—what's done is done—but you can pay the speeding ticket, and your parents have a right to say, "Sorry, but because you have broken our trust in you, it will be a month before you get to use the car again."

I think that when the dust has settled, and you mull it over awhile, you will find grounding appropriate in cases such as these.

When parents ground you, what does it help? It just gets you madder, and then you want to do it again to make them mad.

Take a good hard look at your attitude. You're punishing yourself—and defeating yourself. And you're not helping make your parents any happier, so everybody gets more miserable.

Why don't you just accept the grounding and get on with your life. Who needs to be grounded regularly? That's self-defeating to say the least.

Why are parents so strict with you when you haven't done anything wrong?

Perhaps you haven't done anything wrong because your parents are so strict. If so, you should be thankful. A lot of kids have got hurt because their parents failed to set firm limits with them.

But if you believe your parents are too strict with you, talk to them about it. After all, you have very good grounds for negotiation: you haven't broken any rules, and you haven't done anything wrong.

Try that approach. Perhaps some of the restrictions can be lifted.

Why is it that every time something goes wrong it's my fault?

You're saying you are unfairly blamed. Be honest with yourself and try to determine whether some of those times really were your fault. Are you a person who, whenever you miss a volley in tennis, stops to inspect your racket, or says, "The sun got in my eyes" or "I stumbled on a stone"? If so, perhaps you have the habit of thinking "It's not my fault!" even when it is.

If you have made some mistakes, you'll have to learn to take responsibility for them. You can't have it both ways. Either you're responsible, or you're not. If you want greater freedom, you have to be responsible.

Now, what if you really are being blamed for things you didn't do? In that case you may have parents who are making you a "scapegoat."

Pick a time and place when heads are cool and you're all feeling pretty good. Don't try in the heat of debate and argument; wait until everybody's calmed down and had a little time out. Then say, "I don't understand why I'm being punished when I didn't do what I'm blamed for doing."

If that doesn't work, and your parents really are being totally unfair, then talk to your school counselor about your problems, because your parents may be using you as a lightning rod for other tensions in your home.

How are we supposed to obey and still enjoy being with our parents?

Your question suggests the image of parents giving orders constantly, while you're a storm trooper obeying and saluting every minute. Not many families are run like army posts, although some people do think the military is a wonderful life. Obedience and happiness aren't necessarily mutually exclusive.

A few parents still abide by outmoded principles, such as "Children are to be seen and not heard," and kids must obey, not lead a pleasant life. These attitudes are left over from the "poisonous pedagogy" of the last century, when parents were always right and children were always wrong.

Discuss it with your parents, using some of the methods I've been describing in this book. Most likely you'll find your parents, when they make rules, are trying to nurture you and protect you so you can safely grow up to adulthood.

Are you really talking about putting the dirty dishes in the dishwasher and not leaving them on the table, picking up your clothes and hanging them in your closet, or being back at a certain time when you've gone to a party? Those are legitimate rules, and your obedience will make the household run more smoothly—which should mean greater happiness for everybody, including you.

What do you say to your parents when you come home late?

"I'm sorry, I got home late."

But it's much better to phone your parents before you're due. Parents get scared easily. If you're overdue, they immediately begin thinking, "The car is broken down on a deserted road" or "My child's been kidnapped" or "There's been an accident."

I know, because I've been there as a parent. It's even worse if your parent finally calls the party where you were and discovers you left on time. You may have simply stopped for a hamburger, but the moment you get home, your parents start yelling. The reason they're yelling is they love you.

Perhaps they should be saying, "Wow! Am I glad to see you—why, we called the morgue, the hospital, and the police department. We worried that you were dead in a ditch.

We thought you had been kidnapped and murdered. And now, here you are, safe among us! Come give me a hug!"

But instead they scream, "Where in hell have you been? You're grounded for a month!"

It's their way of saying, "You just tortured us for an hour. And we love you, or we wouldn't have been tortured."

My mother once got really mad because I came in late on a Saturday night. She said next time I was going to be late I should call her. So the next time I called, guess what? She was asleep.

Had you not called, she would have been sitting up waiting for you. Because when you were due home, her mental alarm clock would have awakened her, and then she'd have elbowed your father, and the two of them would have started worrying, and when you finally came home, they'd be yelling.

When you call, your mother knows where you are, that you're responsible, and that you're safe. And knowing that, she can sleep peacefully.

Why do parents have to be so crabby when we do anything wrong?

They may be afraid for you, and fear gets expressed in attack language.

Perhaps they have other worries on their minds, and when you make a mistake, you add to their burden. Your parents might be struggling with money problems, or even health problems. They might not share them with you because they don't want to worry you. But they go around with frowns on their faces and react badly to new upsets.

You should realize you might not know all the facts, and their irritability might not be directed at you.

You might ask them, "Mom, Dad, you've seemed to be a little troubled lately. Is there anything I can do to help?"

Why do adults think teenagers are so troublesome?

Prior to 1940 there wasn't a teenager on earth; at age twelve, kids were usually patted on the head and sent out into the world to work. Parents didn't have to cope with them.

But in 1940 Franklin Delano Roosevelt invented teenagers when he signed the Child Labor Law. Young people who had been employed were now unemployable. So they were put into high schools, which were the warehouses we built for them. Parents were made legally responsible for kids until the age of sixteen, seventeen, or eighteen, depending on the state.

Before 1940 young people were finding out who they were, asserting their freedom, individuality, independence, and judgment in the world. Now they do it in the home.

Parents are obligated to try to see to it that their kids reach adulthood alive, that they don't dope themselves up, become pregnant or get someone else pregnant, or contract a sexually transmitted disease, that they don't kill themselves in an auto accident or die of a drug overdose or a suicidal depression.

So there are bound to be points of tension and conflict. Parents will sometimes find themselves groaning about dealing with a teenager, and teenagers will find themselves groaning about dealing with a parent.

However, the groaning is a lot like that of a woman giving birth. It means new life is coming. If you have handled your teenage years as constructively as you can, and if you have been as understanding of your parents' problems as you expect them to be of yours, you will find that once you reach maturity, you will have a much more beautiful relationship with your parents.

How should you handle your parents after you have done something they do not approve of and you get caught?

You've got the situation reversed. They are trying to figure out how to handle you at that point. You should be as honest and straightforward as you can and then help your parents work out discipline that is fitting for what you did wrong.

We all know that when we've done something wrong we need to balance the books. If we try to get away with it, we we carry guilt around with us, or else we get the notion we won't be caught. The prisons are full of people who think they can get away with wrongdoing.

What do you do when you break something expensive?

You figure out how you're going to replace it.

Parents always yell at you for staying on the phone too long because it costs so much. All of the calls I make are local. We also have call-waiting, so they don't miss calls. When I ask why they want me off the phone, they say, "Because I said so." What kind of answer is that?

Not a very good answer. But your parents may want to make outgoing calls, and that's what is irritating them. When four or five of my kids were teenagers at the same time, I found that every time I lifted my phone, one of the kids was on an extension.

I got tired of saying, "Get off the line, I've got an important call" or "Please don't use the phone, I'm expecting a call" and hampering their social life that way.

Perhaps your family can afford to install another phone, especially if you bear the brunt of your own monthly bills. That way your parents' phone would be left free for them, and you would have your own. That's how we resolved the situation in my home.

If you can work out an arrangement like that, your parents and you will save a lot of energy that's now being wasted.

Is it hard to bring your children up the right way?

There is probably no more difficult task in the world.

Our culture, and television, exert an influence—often negative—far more powerful than the school system. Popular heroes and, in particular, teenage idols often have self-destructive lifestyles (and many of them soon do self-destruct, only to be replaced by others).

The pressures kids feel from their peers seem like a tidal wave, and though this may be scary to you, it's even scarier to your parents.

And then your parents are themselves still trying—just like you—to adjust to an environment changing more rapidly than at any time in history. That makes it hard for them to know how to do the right thing.

How do they discipline their child and not rouse resentment and rebellion? How do they become friends with their child and yet maintain authority, so that they can help their child discern right from wrong? How do they help build their child's self-esteem, when everywhere out there people with low self-esteem are urging more and more drugs and premature sexual behavior and other "remedies" for the tensions of the moment?

If pubescence is a hairy time, being the parent of a pubescent is hairier. Because the parent bears the responsibility for raising that youngster. With so many dangers on the loose, the difference between protecting you and being overcautious is difficult to see and has to be worked out day by day.

The wonderful thing about it, though, is that if the parent handles it properly, it becomes a challenging and growing time. By listening, paying attention, and sharing in some of their enthusiasms, I learned a lot about what was going on in the current world from my kids. At the same time I was able to share my insights into what was good and what was bad, for them, in the world.

Today, with my youngest just nineteen, I can say I learned a lot from raising them, which means they raised me, too. On family occasions, I delight in the community of loving people we created together.

3

Family Affairs

3

I know I love my family, but I know I don't like them at times. Am I bad to feel this way?

No. Loving people and liking them are not the same thing. If you love your family, it means you are committed to your family's good; you want to do anything you can to help them be happy. But there may be times when members of your family do things of which you disapprove, things that disappoint, anger, or upset you; at such times you may not like them very much.

Many people confuse loving and liking. Liking is a warm, positive feeling that—like all feelings—can come and go.

Loving, on the other hand, is a matter of the will. Love doesn't fluctuate like an emotion but, instead, stays as long as you will it to.

Families, as your question suggests, are where the difference between liking and loving really shows. A marriage is a commitment of love. And although there are times when husbands and wives, as well as children, may not like each other—they may be angry, upset, or disappointed with one another—they still love each other. Love is a kind of decision, a conscious willing of good.

More young people would be spared a lot of pain if they understood that a warm feeling for someone, even sexual feelings, does not mean one loves that person and does not mean one is ready for marriage.

And your occasional anger and dislike for members of your family does not mean your family love is gone.

Why is it that I feel more open around my family when nobody else is around?

We're more intimate with some people than others. We all have a few people with whom we are very intimate—like our families—and others with whom we're less intimate— associates and friends. There are many people with whom we're not intimate at all.

In the small circle of your family, you can reveal your innermost self, because they have your trust. You know they love you. When other people are present, you may feel less free to expose yourself, because you don't know whether they will be for you or against you. Intimacy is a matter of trust. Without mutual trust intimacy cannot exist.

I would say, from your question, your feeling of intimacy with your family is at a proper level.

What do you do when you don't want to do as many things with your parents or go as many places as you did when you were younger, but they still want you to?

If your parents are letting go in the proper sense and allowing you more freedom as you mature, they should not demand that you participate in so many of their activities.

Sometimes you should go along to keep your parents happy—there's nothing wrong with that. And your parents probably feel you should share certain activities as a family member.

If you're sixteen years old and your parents don't want to leave you alone all weekend, you probably will have to do as they say. If they're visiting Grandma, maybe you should go for Grandma's sake—she isn't going to be there forever. Later, when she's gone, you'll be thankful you got to know her.

At any rate, the matter of which events are obligatory and which are not is a negotiable issue.

It seems as if I always get used as a handy tool to fulfill all my parents' needs and requests while they just lie back and relax. Is that fair?

I doubt your parents simply give orders from their recliners while you slave around the house all day. I suspect they're paying the mortgage, car loan and insurance, as well as fixing your meals and keeping the lights on and the oil furnace running. In short, they are taking care of your needs in many ways.

Your parents have earned their moments of relaxation. Why not show your appreciation by doing the things they ask?

What should you do if your parents make a rule that you think is unfair?

Tell them, "All right, I think it's unfair, but I'll do it." And then abide by the rule and don't resist it.

Some things in life *are* unfair. When we live in communities, which is what a family is, there are rules. There are rules in hotels, schools, convents, the army, in movie theaters. You can't yell "fire" when there's no fire, for example.

If you think a rule is unfair, take every opportunity to discuss it. But don't break it arbitrarily, because that just adds conflict to the problem.

What can I do when I feel my own family has rejected me? I'm living in a foster home with another family. I have many strong emotions, about both my new family and my old one. How do I deal with my feelings of love, hate, and rejection?

First, try to understand that your feelings are caused by how you are viewing this situation. There's a famous sketch of a woman printed in many psychology textbooks. If you look at it one way, you get a woman that looks like an old witch; if you look at it another, she appears beautiful and young.

The same thing goes when you view your family. Instead of thinking, "My parents put me in a foster home; they rejected me," you might see that your parents are having troubles but did the best they knew how for you at the time. What you take as rejection might really be an attempt to take care of you.

Second, your foster family is trying to help you. They know they aren't your parents, but they care for you. Many people have nobody who cares for them, and many have no escape from home situations that are intolerable.

Not long ago a seventeen-year-old client came to see me. He was going to commit suicide because of problems at home and at school. Three weeks later when I graduated him from therapy, he said, "Nothing has changed in the details of my life. What has changed is my attitude. And because of that I feel a thousand percent better."

He now knew he was not responsible for troubles in his parent's marriage, and he understood why—because of his being upset—his grades were slumping. Once he began to see those things with new eyes, his feelings of despair went away.

The same thing can happen for you. I strongly urge you to talk to a counselor at school about your feelings. That will help you view the situation from another perspective and help you to see how you can make the best of it. Feelings depend entirely on how you choose to look at things. A fresh new look will get your feelings sorted out, and you'll probably feel much better.

What is a good way to keep family members from bickering and yelling and, instead, get them to enjoy being together?

Many families yell a lot. I've never figured out why they yell so much. Too often, bickering is a habit. People think they can improve one another if they criticize enough. But criticism never improves people; it tears them down.

It's good to remember that you can't change how other people behave; you can only change your own behavior. So, when people bicker, don't contribute. If they yell, don't yell back. That way you'll lower the volume by at least that much. If somebody takes verbal sniper shots at you, say, "I don't really want to indulge in bickering. I'd like this family to be happier."

What you bring to any relationship is you. You're responsible for how you behave on your end of that relationship. If other people want to behave badly, that's their problem.

You can't just demand, "Hey, everybody stop yelling and stop bickering." In family therapy I've gotten people en masse to learn new behavior, but in your own family your contribution will be your refusal to take part in bickering. You may even serve as an example: "And a little child shall lead them."

It seems incredible to me that so many people I know have an unpleasant life at home, whereas mine is great, without many major conflicts. Why is it that so many are at odds with either themselves or their parents?

You're one of the fortunate few I mentioned earlier when I said three or four kids in a class might have good relationships with their parents.

Many conflicts start when adolescence and puberty

bump into parental authority, especially when parents aren't trained in communication skills.

When I went to high school and college, I was taught English (a foreign language because we all spoke American) and public speaking, which I did from behind a podium. Very few families have dinner tables equipped with podiums, and English literature doesn't directly teach how to deal intimately with people, how to have a dialogue.

Now, fortunately, there are programs such as Marriage Encounter and Engaged Encounter, which teach couples how to talk to each other. There are also parenting courses that seek to improve parent-child communications. Some schools are teaching children how to express themselves in ways that I never learned. Some schools even teach tiny tots about transactional analysis.

But most often parents communicate the way their own parents did—which means not very well.

Once a couple came in to see me. On the first visit, the wife pointed her finger at her husband and yelled, "Every time I try to talk seriously, he gets up and leaves the room!"

At that point he looked uncomfortable, so I asked him, "Do you want to get up and leave the room?" and he answered, "You bet your life I do!"

"When did you first decide to get up and leave the room when your wife yelled at you?" I asked.

"When I was about five years old."

His wife almost fell off her chair.

He added, "My parents yelled at each other all the time, and that scared me, so I decided when I grew up and got married, I'd never yell at my wife." That's how he kept the peace in his family: by leaving the room.

But his wife came from a family in which everybody

yelled. She thought yelling was how you communicate important things.

I got her to lower her voice, and her husband was willing to stay in the room.

That's an example of how we pick up our communication skills from the way we were raised and from the way we choose to respond to our family. The husband chose to respond to his parents by leaving the room when they yelled; his wife chose to respond to her parents by imitating them.

How were your parents raised? A father who never hugs probably comes from a family that never touched. A father who never says "I love you" probably never heard his father say it to him.

Some families communicate by bickering; others, by teasing one another. For still others, there is a lot of superficial dialogue that avoids intimacy. There are many different family styles.

In your case, apparently, your parents learned how to communicate well. They keep the channels of communication open; they talk rationally; they express their feelings and are open to your feelings. Count your lucky stars. You're learning how to communicate well, too. Maybe you should become a therapist and teach other people how to do it.

How can I cope with Victorian parents?

If they're Victorian, you've probably buried them. Otherwise, they'd be about a hundred years old.

By "Victorian," do you mean that you can't discuss sex with them? If so, you'll have to educate them about the world out there, but do it gradually. Do you mean they're strict about how late you can stay out and things like that?

Then you'll have to discuss and negotiate with them.

The point is, labeling people doesn't help you understand them, and it certainly doesn't help you and your parents resolve your differences.

The first way of dealing with "Victorian" parents is to understand they're not Victorian, they're simply who they are. Labeling people is a dead end. It boxes them—and you —in. Find out why they hold the standards they do, what they're afraid of, what their motives are. Understanding them will be your best first step toward coping with them.

How can I get my parents to trust me?

By proving you're trustworthy. Now, perhaps your parents distrust everybody. If so, you might not be able to get your parents to trust you; just be yourself.

More likely, though, you have broken their trust. All of us are allowed a few lapses, but broken trust is difficult to repair. If you lied once, how do your parents know you're not lying now?

If that has happened, the only way you can regain their trust over the next few weeks and months is by consistently proving you are trustworthy again.

A novelist friend of mine told me about the time he arrived at school without his lunch. He didn't want to admit he'd forgotten his lunch, so he told his teacher he had met a hungry man huddling in the doorway during the rainstorm outside. He said he gave the man his lunch. The teacher was so impressed she got up in front of the class and announced that he had done a wonderful thing. His classmates piled cookies, fruit, and sandwiches on his desk; the teacher got some juice from the teacher's lounge. He was the hero of the class because he had been so generous to the impoverished man. Just then his mother came into the classroom with his lunch and chided him for leaving it on the kitchen table.

From that time on, if he came into class dripping, his shoes overflowing with water, and said to the teacher, "It's raining out," she would go over to the window, open it, and put out her head before she'd believe him.

Trust is earned. It's too precious for any of us to treat casually or break lightly.

How do we get my father to knock off his vulgar language, which upsets the whole household?

Your father probably learned to swear from his father. Perhaps he thinks it's macho to shock the household and keep it upset. It's possible he's expressing deep anger, low self-esteem.

You can't change him on your own. But if you, your brothers, and your sisters go to your mother, she may have the leverage to persuade him his language is distressing everybody.

If he still can't stop cursing, it means he's compulsive about it and needs a therapist's help to find out why he likes to assert his power with foul language.

Do you think it's good for teenagers to work around the home?

Not only good, but necessary. That's especially true in families in which both parents work outside the home (as in the majority of American households).

Most people learn how to cook, make a bed, and vacuum a floor at home. If they don't they tend to be rather ineffectual spouses later on.

Before 1928 most kids lived on farms. They earned their keep from the time they could toddle. They fed the chickens, picked up the firewood, brought the cows in and milked them, and helped peel the potatoes.

Most of us don't live on farms anymore, and we have a lot of labor-saving gadgets. But there's still work to be done. There are still kitchen floors to be mopped and potatoes to be peeled, the garbage to go out, the lawn to be cut.

If you want more freedom and autonomy, you have to share in the responsibility of the household, too. Who said fathers and mothers must be servants to their children? That only parents can take out the garbage, and wash the dishes? You use the bathroom; why not help clean it up?

If you volunteer for some of these chores, you'll delight your parents. They'll find you a more responsible person and will probably reward you with more liberty. You'll also enjoy the feeling of being a more fully contributing member of the family.

Shouldn't your parents give you respect and include you in making family decisions?

Every human being, from the tiniest to the biggest and oldest, deserves respect as a person.

If you're talking about where your family is going camping this year, then your parents should, and probably do, respect your opinion.

But families are not, and never were intended to be, democracies. Somebody has to make fundamental decisions for the survival of your family.

Whether Mom or Dad takes a new job in Chicago is a decision between your mother and father. You can rest assured that they're taking your needs into account. But you can't really help make that sort of decision, because you don't have the experience necessary to have an informed opinion, and you are not ultimately responsible for the family's welfare.

Why is it that one parent is often much more protective than the other one?

Often a mother is more protective than a father. On the other hand, some fathers are more protective of their daughters. It varies from family to family. Much depends upon a parent's personal history and life experience.

People have different points of view. You're going to have to learn to cope with that fact all your life, so you may as well begin now.

How do I get my parents to be my friends?

By being friendly. Some kids believe the way to assert independence is by rebelling. But rebellion is unfriendly.

If you are still living at home, your parents have authority. Your status is unequal, and when they use their authority, that difference in roles puts friendship aside momentarily.

But as you grow in wisdom and age, your relationship will change. There's a gradual letting go, a gradual shift in emphasis. When finally you take authority over your own life, you and your parents, if you've been handling things well, will be true friends. It's a gradual progression that is meant to occur naturally.

Unfortunately, some parents hold on too tightly; their kids may react self-destructively or rebelliously, and they don't end up friends. Some parents or kids have problems with alcohol or drugs; things end in confrontation, anger, upset, and uproar—anything but friendliness.

But you can't go wrong by keeping the channels of communication open from your end and by being as friendly as you can be. Share your experiences with them. Be interested in their experiences.

How do you get your parents to smile or laugh?

Tickle them under the arms. Bring home a joke from school. On Mother's Day or Father's Day give them a book of Gary Larson comics or Bill Cosby's book on parenting.

Perhaps your parents are struggling with something you don't know about—a problem in their marriage, or your grandmother's illness, or something on the job.

Or it's possible your parents are simply dour by temperament; perhaps they came from families that failed to teach them that life is meant to be enjoyed.

At any rate, you can't really change your parents. Your concern is your own attitude. Try to be as cheerful as you can despite their dourness. And when you see a chance, inject a little fun into your family life.

Sometimes I get very angry over something that's happened at school or with my friends. Then I let it out with my family. How can I keep my anger from coming out like that?

There are all kinds of ways to handle anger. You can take it out on your younger brother or sister, kick your dog, throw things around your room. That's called displacement, and it only makes things worse.

Or you can try to hold your anger in. That's called repression, and it can damage your innards—and it may explode later.

The best way is to come home and talk it out. Say to your mother or father, "I'm really upset about something that happened at school today. I'm angry because so-and-so did this and that." You'll feel better, you won't be taking your anger out on other people, and your parents will know you aren't angry at them.

If your anger continues to trouble you, pick up *The Angry*

Book, by Theodore Isaac Rubin, M.D. It describes the many ways people handle or mishandle their anger.

What is a good brother or sister?

One who builds up your self-esteem, doesn't put you down, cares about you, may even help you with your homework. You can talk about things with a brother or sister like that, knowing your confidences will be respected.

My mom is always taking my younger sister shopping, and she has a "pals" kind of relationship with her. But with me and my other sister, Mom is serious and often says she doesn't have time to go shopping. How can kids deal with parents who are showing favoritism?

That's very painful for you. Favoritism does occur in families, and sometimes parents don't realize they're acting that way. Perhaps that's true of your mother.

You and your sister should sit down alone with your mother and tell her how you feel as clearly, calmly, and nonthreateningly as you can.

Tell her, "When you take Sis to the store, and you treat her this way and that way, I feel very hurt because you don't do that with me. I could be wrong, but sometimes I think that's favoritism." And so on.

Talk only about your feelings and your thoughts. Don't judge her. Admit openly you could be wrong. That way you open the door for her to express her feelings freely and to agree with you (or not to agree with you).

If you attack, she will counterattack and close up. She simply may have different ideas and feelings about what she's doing. Give her a chance to know what you are feeling.

You'll have to be very clear and as objective as you can. Don't allow your discussion to develop into an argument or a name-calling match. Grant that you could be wrong, because your perception is based only on your seeing, your feelings; that enables her to talk to you without feeling threatened.

If she adamantly denies she plays favorites, and she continues, you may just have to accept it. And if it becomes even more painful, talk to a counselor or teacher. You don't want this problem to affect your sense of self-worth.

Now, as a parent of eight children, I know that at times some kids are more likable than others; some are easier to get along with than others, some create more problems; some are endearing and charming, others are more difficult to reach.

But that says nothing about their worth as people and as children. I once described my family as a garden in which grew a rose, a cactus, a lavender plant, a lilac, some dahlias, and some chrysanthemums; they're all different, but they each shed beauty and their own light in the family relationship. They're each unique and uniquely lovable.

That's true of you and your sister, too.

How do you stop a brother from teasing a younger sister?

If you're an older brother or sister, try to reason with him at a time when he's quiet. Don't argue or fight, but get him to sit down. Ask him, "Why do you like to tease your younger sister? What do you feel when you tease her?" Try to find out why he does it. Then try to get him to understand what it does to his sister. "How would you feel if someone did that to you?"

Then point out you and everyone else would be happier with him if he stopped. His younger sister would like him, and people wouldn't feel angry with him all the time.

If he's the middle child, teasing may be his way of attracting attention, even negative attention. He might be jealous; he might want to hurt his sister because he feels she's getting more attention.

Yelling at him won't help. The best thing to do is to give him lots of positive attention when he behaves well. If he makes it through dinner without teasing his sister, afterwards tell him, "Boy, I really liked the way you behaved this evening at dinner and how nice you were to your sister."

Positive attention like that usually goes much further toward solving the problem than criticism when he's behaving badly.

Why does my brother pick on me? I am eleven and my brother is thirteen.

When people in families behave badly, they're sometimes really saying, "Hey, I'm me, and I'm here—pay attention to me!" In other words, your brother may be picking on you so he can inflate his own importance. Perhaps he feels your parents are giving you more attention than they give to him, and he's angry about that.

Quietly, without his knowledge, chat with your mother about him. Find out what she thinks. Let her know how it pains you. Don't do it in a tearful, angry way, but take her aside and say, "Can I have a few minutes with you alone?" Sit down with her and say, "You know, this is what's going on, and I don't know what to do about it. I really like my older brother, and I don't want you to punish him for this, but I don't know what to do. I just want to understand what's going on, and I want you to know. Maybe you could talk to him a little bit." Something like that.

Do it as peacefully as you can, and you might bring more peace to your home that way.

Since I'm older (16) Mom lets my brother pick the work he wants to do and I get stuck with the rest, the least favorite work. I'm supposed to be mature about it, but it makes me mad. How can I tell her I need different rules?

If your little brother is very little, your mother is just trying to get him used to chores. If he's only a year or two younger than you, you should discuss the problem with your mother.

First, stop grumbling. Do your work well, not in a way that shows how angry you are. Then choose a neutral time and corner, when your little brother isn't around, and say, "I want to talk for a few minutes without interruption and just tell you some feelings I've been having and some thoughts I've been having. Then I'll be quiet and you can tell me how you feel about what I said."

My hunch is your previous debates have taken place just after you've been given a chore to do, and your mother sees your objections as reluctance to do the chore. And probably your mother responds by saying, "Because I said so!"

Another debate won't help; you want a discussion. Wait until after the chore is done, and then, after you're calm and you've sorted out your own feelings clearly, start.

How do I get my parents to let me do as much as my older brother does, like going out?

This is always a difficult problem in a family of several children. Differences in age do matter. Your parents must match up the degree of freedom they give you with your emotional, intellectual, and physical maturity. I know it's hard to accept when you're, say, fourteen, and your seventeen-year-old brother gets to do more things.

But your parents are wise. Your older brother has more

privileges because he also has more responsibilities. When you get to be the age your brother is now, you'll probably have the same freedoms—and the same responsibilities.

My older sister talks back to my parents and they get mad, and then whatever we do, they get mad at us. And then everyone is mad.

First, avoid confrontations with your parents after your older sister has had one.

It might be useful if you younger ones discuss among yourselves this pattern of behavior. You've described a regular setup, and you don't want to play into that setup anymore. So among yourselves decide that the next time this happens, none of you will involve yourself in an argument with your parents. That will cool that problem right away.

When you get involved, your parents displace their anger on you. If you keep out of it, maybe things will happen differently. Perhaps there will be a different chemistry between your parents and older sister, and—if you don't deflect their attention—they might even resolve their disputes.

You can make an even more positive contribution by going as a kind of committee to your older sister and saying, "You know, when you fight with them, that makes all of us get hurt."

And if you've noticed that those arguments between your sister and parents begin with "attack language" like "you always, you never, you ought, you don't" then perhaps you can suggest that she find some other way of expressing herself.

The problem with attack language is that it always causes the other person to counterattack.

Perhaps you can advise your sister to start not with "you always, you never, you ought, you don't" but with "I feel." She has a right to express her feelings. (And I don't mean disguised attack language like "I feel you always, you never, you ought, you don't").

Your older sister's fights might be her way of expressing her anger over what's going on in life, or of seeking to break loose from your parents.

Don't you become party to that. Get off the field, and leave that battleground to them. You're responsible only for *your* relationship to your parents. If that means you decide to go quietly to your room and read a book or watch TV, fine. Don't tangle with those three when they're agitated.

Ever since my brother was born, my dad hasn't paid much attention to me. What should I do? I tried to talk to him, but it didn't help.

Your mother is your best ambassador to your father. She may be able to convey your message more meaningfully than you could.

When you can't talk to one parent, then express your feelings later to the other. Say, "I tried to talk to Daddy about this, and he wouldn't listen, and he hasn't behaved any differently. I just want to tell you how neglected I feel since the baby was born. Is there anything I can do or you can do to help Daddy pay attention to me?"

Attention is a sign of love. We all need attention, and when we don't get it the right way, some of us do things that get it the wrong way. You don't want to start that.

With twelve children in the family, I sometimes feel that I don't get enough attention from my parents. What is a good way to get your mom and dad's attention so you can just sit for a few minutes and talk?

That is a problem in large families. As the father of eight, I tried to spend time with my kids during the course of my normal duties. If I was walking to the post office, I would say, "Mark, would you like to walk to the post office with me?" We could talk on the way to the post office and back.

Or if I was going to the grocery store, I would say, "Jennifer, would you like to go to the grocery store with me?"

You can do this, too. The next time your mother is taking off for the supermarket, ask, "Can I go along?" When your father is mowing the lawn, go out and ask, "Can I help?" With twelve children in your family, your parents have a lot of things to do, and though that doesn't give them much time to give their kids individual "sit and talk" attention, it does give you opportunities to help them—and find time to chat that way.

Why are parents, especially fathers, more lenient with sons than with daughters?

A boy walking down the street is not likely to be pulled into the bushes and raped. On a date a boy is more able physically to protect himself from being taken advantage of sexually. And sons don't get pregnant.

Even though the boy is just as responsible as the girl, the burden of pregnancy falls mainly on the girl. Some fathers even believe "Boys will be boys" and excuse a boy's sexual exploits because he's not going to come back pregnant.

That's not fair, but it is a reality in our culture. Statistics on rape, pregnancy, and sexually transmitted disease (which often affects girls more seriously) document problems that are very real. I describe some of these in more detail in the chapter on sexuality.

4

Can We Talk?

4

It seems like whenever we sit down at the table for dinner my teenage sister starts disagreeing with my parents about something trivial, and then pretty soon it's a big shouting match. I know they love each other, so why do these fights start?

Have you noticed that those arguments between your sister and parents begin with "attack language" like "you always, you never, you ought, you don't"?

Teenagers, particularly, tend to generalize into "always" statements. But with emotions running hot, attack language always causes the other person to counterattack.

"You" language is almost always attack language unless it is "You are beautiful. You are lovely. You're terrific."

I have no right to say "you always" do this or that; what I should say, instead, is that when you do this or that, it affects me in a certain way. I have a right to my feelings and, in a loving family context, a right to express my feelings.

If you can, take your sister aside sometime and gently suggest she find a different way of discussing issues with your parents. Because the arguments are started by your sister over "trivial" things, I would guess there are larger issues she needs to talk to somebody about, maybe she should see her school counselor.

What's the right way to argue with your parents?

Lovingly. Always keep in mind that you love your parents and they love you. If you do that, you'll be more patient with one another and more likely to listen as well as talk.

You don't really want an argument. What you want is a greater understanding of one another, so you and your parents can work out some sort of negotiated settlement.

And it's useful to remember you cannot discuss something seriously if you're both standing, on the move, or about to go out. You hear better when you're sitting. The best thing to do is take your mother or father by the hand and say, "Can you sit down here for a minute? I'd like to talk to you. It might take five minutes. Do you have five minutes to talk?" When they sit down, continue, "I'd like to talk for a minute and then I'll shut up and listen to you."

Go ahead and explain your point, and then, as you promised, shut up and listen. Don't interrupt.

Another good technique is to try to tell the other person what you heard before you jump in with a response to what you thought you heard. It's easy to misunderstand what the other person has said, particularly when discussing an emotionally charged issue.

Research suggests that most people use five hundred basic words for most of their conversation. But for those five hundred words there are fourteen thousand varying dictionary definitions. That means there are about twenty-eight definitions per word; therefore, your odds of correctly understanding what someone has just said are only about one in twenty-seven. That's why it's useful for you to respond, "If I hear you correctly, you're telling me this . . ." Get every statement clear before you move on to your response.

One of the greatest barriers to communication is that we talk too much. We jump to conclusions and make emotional statements that have little to do with the real issues.

If you sit down, ask questions instead of talk, and really try to find out what your parents meant before you respond, you'll find you talk to your parents more constructively.

What do you say to a parent who has a bad habit that bugs you?

If it's a lifelong habit, you may not be able to break your parent of it. If Daddy has spit in the fireplace all his life, there's not much you can do except register your dismay at his using fireplaces as spittoons.

You do have a right to comment on a bad habit if it is injurious or unsanitary. But you can't expect to change people.

Even as a therapist, I can't change people. Rather, I help them change themselves. I help them change their marriages, their personal lives, even their bad habits. But it is they who do the changing. In fact, they've already done half the work of changing when they make their first appointment with me, because it means they've really decided they want to change.

What you can do is offer your feelings and insights about Daddy's or Mommy's drinking, smoking, or using the fireplace as a spittoon. But you can't hope your parents will instantly jump up and cry, "Oh! I'll stop spitting in the fireplace—or smoking, or drinking—right now!" Only they can make that decision, when they choose to.

Why does my father get mean when he's losing an argument? He won't admit he's wrong. He shouts and threatens. He's always got to win.

Your father apparently believes arguments are to be won or lost. So, whatever you do, don't argue with him, because he'll always try to win no matter what the issue. When your father thinks he's losing, he'll resort to attack language, and that puts you on the defensive. Eventually he "wins," and he's finally satisfied he put down the upstart.

You want a discussion, not an argument. When he tries to start an argument, you say, "Dad, I wouldn't mind discussing this, but I don't want to argue."

That goes for marriages, too, by the way. There never should be win-lose arguments in a marriage. If you win, you've proved you're married to a loser. If you lose, you resent the blazes out of the other person. That's why arguments are a bad idea.

It's much better to have discussions, in which you can share insights with one another and thus gain a better mutual understanding. Arguments are a waste of time and energy and only hurt relationships.

Whenever I talk with my dad, he talks and I listen. He never praises me for something good, just puts me down for something bad.

He was probably raised with constant criticism himself. That's not unusual. In one recent survey, teachers reported they spent 70 to 80 percent of their time commenting negatively on students' work rather than positively. Unfortunately, the same goes for many parents; they think they're going to correct you by pointing out flaws.

Parents and teachers don't understand that you would correct the flaws yourself if they would only praise your accomplishments. There's strong scientific evidence for that.

Parents often take good behavior for granted and pay attention only to the bad. But attention is a sign of love. So what happens? Some kids, especially younger ones, start thinking unconsciously that they're loved when they do bad things, because that's when they get attention.

In your case, the next time your father lists the things you've done wrong, ask him, "Do you recall anything I did right last week?" Be prepared for a dumb answer, at first, because you'll take him by surprise. And don't do this in a smart-alecky fashion: you want to try this gently.

If he does all the talking, and you have difficulty responding, perhaps you can ask permission to speak. There are various ways of doing that. When he's through, you can say, "Are you through?" When he answers yes, you say, "Do I have permission to respond to some of that?" or "Would you listen if I have a few things to say?" If he says no, drop it.

Chances are, if you try this politely, and long enough, one day he'll say yes. That's when you can start to respond. If he interrupts, wait patiently for him to finish. Then you say, "May I continue my response?"

Raising parents is really tough. If your father's father treated him the way he's treating you, your father probably thinks that's how parents are supposed to be.

But if you follow my suggestions politely and respectfully, you may even teach your father how to have a dialogue.

My father was raised to believe that at the dinner table nobody spoke unless spoken to, especially children. Well, he had nine boys and a girl in his family, and I was his seventh son. I talk a lot. The poor man nearly went out of his mind, because we all talked at once.

If you do it gently and respectfully, you may actually turn your father around.

I have many secrets from my mom. I'd like to tell her about them, but I don't know how to start or if she'd just get mad and worry.

It is very good you want to share these things with your mother. The best way to start is to choose a time when the two of you are alone and aren't going to be interrupted by the phone or the doorbell or somebody coming home. Perhaps you can accompany her to the supermarket. When you're in the car, say, "Mom, I wanted to come along because I wanted to tell you something, and I hope you won't get upset, but I'd like to find out how you feel about this."

Pick a small thing you feel pretty safe with. Ask for her advice and insight. Or ask, "What would you do about . . .?" See what happens.

If it fails, and your mother puts up barriers (some mothers are frightened of what they might learn), then you might have to say, "Well, I really would like to share a lot more stuff with you. But when you react that way it shuts me down." Try again some other time.

But if it succeeds, you can move to the next one. You might say, "It's been wonderful to talk with you, can we find time to do it again sometime?"

How do I tell my mother I am not a little girl anymore without upsetting her?

"Mom, I'm not a little girl any more." That's probably the best way to begin. Pick a time you're alone with her, driving to school or the market. If the radio's off, the car can be a nice isolation booth. Your mother can handle traffic automatically, and you can get a chance to chat.

If your conversation upsets her, maybe she would like to keep you a little girl. As you grow up, it means she's losing her role as mother. Some mothers find that distressing.

You might try, "Mom, how do you see me these days? How grown up do you see me?" Or "Mom, when you were fifteen, sixteen, seventeen, how did you feel toward your parents?" Or "Mom, when you were sixteen, how did you handle boys who made passes at you?"

These questions might help you get to know each other better.

If she gets defensive, and sternly asks, "Why do you bring up that question?" you can answer, "Because I need some advice from you. I'm at the age when boys make passes, you know?" Then she has to recognize you're growing up.

It requires courage, but the direct approach is probably the best.

What do you do when you're discussing things with your parents and you start to win, so they bring up other areas in your life that you're not doing so hot at?

In our culture winning is everything; when people begin to lose, they will do anything to get an advantage. They will bring things out of the past to hit you with; they'll deflect the argument to things that have little to do with the issue.

Stay out of win-lose arguments. Unless you're a member of the American Bar Association and standing before a judge, winning and losing arguments has no place in your life. In your family, you should be looking for better understanding, not for who's right or wrong.

If someone is going to be right, the other person has to be wrong. But nobody wants to be wrong—not you, not your brother, not your mother, not your father.

What you all want is to understand one another, support one another, help one another grow up in love. That's what families and family communications should be.

The moment you see a win-lose argument coming, say, "Sorry, I no longer engage in win-lose arguments; I was just looking for some understanding," and drop the issue.

Is it necessary for a teenager to tell her parents everything about her day, her life, and her feelings? I call it an invasion of privacy when my parents try to pry, and they say I'm closing myself off.

All parents and teenagers must strike the delicate balance between privacy and communication.

Some parents don't talk enough to their children, claiming they're respecting their kids' privacy. But they're actually avoiding their kids' problems and sweeping them under the rug.

Meanwhile, other parents, like yours, perhaps—in seeking to keep the dialogue open—may behave more like inquisitors than friends. They grill you: "What'd you do today? Who'd you see at lunch? Where'd you go?" and so on.

If you look at it that way, you may see that your parents' motives are good; they're just handling the situation awkwardly.

Tell them, "When I come home I sometimes feel as though I'm being given the third-degree. I know you get a little nervous about me as I go through this stage in my life, but let's make an agreement: I'll tell you the important things I want to share with you, because I trust you. When you give me the third-degree I want to clam up."

Put it in your own words, but try to reassure your parents you're not closing yourself off, you just don't like the close questioning. And remember, they are showing an interest in you and trying to keep communication going.

How do you persuade your parents to let you do something that is really not a major thing, like piercing your ears?

I sometimes have trouble understanding why parents choose battlegrounds over things like this, nonessentials. A ring in your nose, I might draw a line at, but pierced ears is not a capital issue.

But if your parents are adamant, and you're still living at home, then probably you're going to have to follow their judgment. And it's not worth a big fight on your part, either; you don't really have to be just like everybody else.

Find out if your mother has pierced ears. Many women do. If she does, quietly ask her why it is okay for her but not for you. Or ask her at what age she thinks it's okay for you. Maybe she'll say, "On your seventeenth birthday you can have pierced ears," and then at least you have that to look forward to.

You will just have to negotiate issues like this as best as you can. If your parents are laying down the law, you're better off not making a major case out of what is a minor item; you'll waste a lot of energy.

How can I get money out of my parents? How can you say the right words?

The best way I know of getting money is to earn it. Why not apply at a fast-food restaurant, the kind that is always looking for help, and get a job?

If you can't find a job after school, perhaps you can negotiate an allowance in return for doing chores at home.

Don't expect "Gimme" to do it. Nothing's free; your father or your mother have to earn every penny, and maybe they're stretching themselves even now in order to meet the family budget. They may not have enough left over to hand out money for records or things like that.

How can I convince my parents to get me a car?

Why convince them? Why not start saving your money? That's the normal way. Then you can be very proud of earning your own car, paying the insurance and gas bills.

This question, like the preceding, implies, "My parents owe me a car; they owe me money." But that's not true.

Yes, many parents do give their children cars, money, and all kinds of material things. But many of them do so because they don't want to give their children time, attention, or care.

One of my clients was born wealthy, but she was in great pain because her parents never showed her any love; they just dumped things on her.

It can be very loving for a parent to encourage a child to earn that stereo or car. When one of my sons dropped out of college and came home, I told him he would have to pay board and room.

He was very upset about that, so I said, "Oh, I don't need your money, but you need to pay it. In fact, if you think I just want your money, you can watch me put it down the kitchen disposal. I would not be a loving father unless I helped you to learn your responsibilities; among them is that food and housing have to be paid for."

So he paid board and room for six months (no, I didn't have to put it down the disposal), found himself a better job, and got his own apartment. He is now married. We're good friends. He doesn't resent the fact that I taught him some sense of responsibility.

How do I talk my parents into letting me go to places that I know are safe but they don't think are safe?

Ask them, "Where did you hang out when you were kids?" Some hung out in record shops. When I was young, record shops had booths in which you could play the records to see if you were going to buy them. We used to play twenty or thirty records for every one we bought. Others hung out at the drugstore or the park.

Of course, if your parents grew up in the country, maybe all they did on a summer's evening was walk down the road and watch a neighbor's corn grow. Anything more than that is scary for them.

Your parents are probably trying to protect you. What you need to do is find out what they're scared of and try to allay those fears.

Perhaps you can say to them, "Hey, come on down. I want you to see this place. Come with me." That may be a bit embarrassing to you, but if you take them down and stroll through the mall with them, and say, "See, this is what's going on. The kids just sit around here and talk, and they go over there and they get a soda. You know, we just shoot the breeze." Maybe their fears will disappear.

How do you deal with parents who don't want to listen to what you have to say?

I have found—at whatever age—that the person who says, "Hey, Mom and Dad, I really love you, and I just want to talk to you a little bit, will you listen?" usually gets listened to.

If you've asked very politely, in the context of love, and they're too neurotic, scared, or character-disordered to listen, then you've got problem parents. You may have to talk to another adult for help.

Go in to see a counselor at school, and say, "I've got a problem at home. My parents won't listen to me, and I've got to talk to an adult about this and that." Ask for some pointers on how to handle the problem.

There are many willing adults around, especially in the school system, who are qualified to counsel you and serve as intermediaries with parents. Often parents come in and say, "We don't know how to handle Jane or Joe, and we want your help," and Jane or Joe has already been in because of difficulties in raising them.

What's the best way to tell your parents that you're in trouble and need some help?

Say, "Sit down, Mom and Dad, I've got to talk to you. It's very serious. I'm in trouble, and I need your help." The direct approach is always best.

Your mother bore you in her womb for nine months, and your father celebrated your birth. They have been proud of you, and they have invested an awful lot of energy and love in you. They aren't going to disown you because you have made a mistake or got into some sort of trouble.

Kids have become pregnant, come down with a sexually transmitted disease, developed an alcohol or drug problem or gotten into other trouble and predicted their parents would react with horror and revulsion, dynamite the house, and leave the state. But when they've told their parents, they've found themselves given a hug or an arm around the shoulder, and told, "Well, you're really in a mess, and we'll just have to see what we can do to get you out of it."

There are parents who disown children who do not live up to their inordinate expectations, of course, but those parents never loved their child to begin with. Fortunately, such parents are the rare exception.

If your parents show any concern for you, I think you can trust them with serious business. It is when they find out that you haven't trusted them with your trouble that they are really hurt. Problems can even bring families closer together.

If they let you down, go to a counselor at school, a teacher you respect, or an aunt, uncle, or grandparents.

Don't think you have to struggle through a serious problem all alone.

But remember, your parents are usually your first and best asset.

How do I know if my parents love me?

If you love your parents, you're probably returning the love they've shown you.

Some parents are not articulate about love. One client of mine had never heard her father say he loved her. When she asked him why not, he said, "I can't." He was unaccustomed to putting his feelings into words.

Such parents try to show their love in other ways. One way is by trying to see you're well fed, well housed, and well clothed and that your dental and medical bills are paid. One father said, "Well, of course I love my son John—do you think I would have paid all these bills and worked my tail off if I didn't love him?" He thought actions spoke louder than words.

But most of us need to hear the words. You might just have to go up to them on an appropriate occasion and ask, "I love you—do you love me?" See what happens.

Here's another idea: Send your mother a little gift or surprise on a day other than Mother's Day. Do the same for your father on a day other than Father's Day. You may find that will help open them up.

How can you tell your parents that you love them when those words aren't used frequently in your household?

On Thursday, out of the blue, mail a card to your dad's office. Write on it something like, "I was thinking of you and wanted you to know how special you are in my life."

In October give a Valentine card to your mother. Write

on it, "I know it's not Valentine's Day, but I wanted you to know I love you." Or give her a rose, or send your father a trinket. Or give them both breakfast in bed one Saturday morning.

Parents need all the encouragement they can get. And a lot of parents wonder if their kids care for them. A lot of parents would love to hear their youngsters say "I love you." Parents wonder if they're doing a good job, if they're respected, if the kids are accepting them.

This may surprise you, but inside every parent is a teenager, or even a little kid, who wonders, "Am I really adequate to be a parent?"

If every week or two you took the risk of saying, one way or another, "I love you," you'd be doing a wonderful thing for your family and yourself.

How do I tell my dad I want to be independent when I'm scared to death of him?

Independence is coming soon enough. When you graduate from high school you'll have to make some decisions. Do you want go to college? Get a job? Enter the military?

When you do any of these things, you're going to be independent. Independence will take care of itself. You don't have to talk about it a lot.

But your being so scared of your father worries me. What's he do that scares you? Ask yourself why you scare yourself with him. If he's forbidding and aloof, he may have been raised that way.

If so, somebody's got to break the shell. If you're the one who recognizes the shell is there, perhaps you should take your courage in your hands and let him know through tokens of esteem, or through a few words here or there, that you really care about him. It might be very helpful.

The only thing that drives out fear is love. And maybe you'll have to be the one to take the first step.

That's part of the task of raising parents in this day and age.

How can I get my parents to understand some of the social pressures confronting teenagers today?

Most parents are very aware of the stress kids are under and wish they knew some way of alleviating it.

Try talking to them about it. They survived being teenagers—although perhaps the pressure was not quite as heavy toward drug and alcohol use or sex as it is nowadays. Send up a trial balloon: "What do you think of that item about crack in the newspaper?" Or "Did you see that TV news story about teenage pregnancy?" You can use these as the basis for talking in general about what's going on and the pressures you're facing.

Or ask your mother while you're washing dishes together, "Do you think the pressures you confronted in high school were as bad as mine?"

She will probably respond, "What pressures are you confronting?" And you can tell her.

You might ask, "What pressures did you feel in high school about virginity or drinking? We get a lot today."

Of course, some youngsters tell me, "I wouldn't dare talk about sex with my mother, she doesn't know anything about it, and she'd run from the room!" Give your mother credit. She probably knows more about sex than you realize.

My parents seem to have no understanding of how I feel or why I act the way I do. Is there a way to talk to them so they understand better?

After school, if your mother's home, go to her and say, "Mom, do you have ten minutes so I can talk with you?" If she says yes, say, "Well, come over here and sit down for a few minutes. I want to talk to you." Then, "I sometimes wonder if you understand what's going on in me, and I really want to open up with you. I love you and I want to be closer to you. Would you just listen to me for a few minutes, and then I'll shut up and you can talk." That always seems to work.

If your mother or father doesn't have the time, you can say, "When can we schedule ten or twenty minutes to talk?"

Once you've scheduled it, sit down—that's very important, remember—and say, "I want to unburden my heart a bit to you. I want to share my feelings with you. I love you very much; that's why I'm trusting you."

Put it in the context of love and trust, and you'll probably strike gold.

How do you keep your parents from lecturing you?

Unfortunately, your parents probably think they're supposed to know everything. I try to tell parents to quit knowing everything and just be human. Lecturing is a lousy way to communicate. It implies the lecturer is talking down to you, a sort of one-way street. Parents should remember we're all human beings in this together.

In your case, try to listen for what's behind the lecture. Is it a concern for your welfare? Is it love? Or is it just somebody being pompous?

Let's say your father has just finished a lecture. Tell him, "If I hear you right, behind all that lecturing, you're worried about whether or not I'm having sex." A response like that will blow the lecture through the wall.

Or, you might say, "Do I hear you correctly, are you trying to tell me you love me?"

Your parents are probably trying to raise you to be

strong, mature, and successful in life. The trouble is, they're doing it the wrong way.

So the best thing you can do is to boil down what they're trying to say into a couple of sentences. Then respond, "Are you trying to tell me that you really care about me? Or that you're really worried about me?" That way you can make it really simple for them.

How can I get my parents to begin talking on an adult level with me, and why do so many parents, like mine, leave their children out of conversations?

Many parents think children are nonpersons and treat them as objects. Some men even treat their wives as objects. The "wife" and "the kids"—so many objects orbiting the circumference of their personal globe. Sometimes they realize these are persons only when they are in danger of losing them.

Your complaint is legitimate if that's how your parents are treating you. If you can respond in a good-humored way —and I don't mean sarcastic, or snarly—you might remind them you are a person.

I once introduced my family to a guest "and here's my tribe." To my great embarrassment, my kids immediately started whooping and performing an Indian war dance around us. Well, I never again called them a "tribe."

Is there any time that it is acceptable to lie to your parents?

Lying strikes at the root of trust in a relationship. Take the example of a daughter of divorced parents whose mother wants her to tell if her father is dating. The daughter is tempted to lie, thinking a lie will stop either parent from being hurt. But her lie will probably be found out, and after that her mother won't trust her as much. That way, everyone gets hurt.

A much better way of handling that problem is to answer "I think you should ask him" or "I'm not going to carry messages; I am not a spy."

Or take the example of a son whose father is prying into his affairs. The son is afraid that what he might divulge will upset his father, so he considers lying. But, again, it's much better to be direct and say "I have a right to privacy" or "I really don't want to discuss that."

I believe lying destroys your ability to have a trusting relationship, and you don't want that to happen. Again and again I have found husbands and wives in therapy who are more shocked that their spouse lied to them than that their spouse was having an affair.

You see, they could understand having an affair, and they could work to heal the wound. But they found it very difficult to forgive a point-blank lie. They would always wonder, "Well, how do I know he or she isn't lying to me now?"

You have a right to your privacy, but don't lie to protect it.

How do you let your parents know that you don't want to do what they want you to do without getting into an argument?

The transition period we know as adolescence, in which you move toward independence, is not always easy. There's bound to be friction as your thrust for independence meets your parents' obligations to set reasonable limits.

You gradually evolve toward independence by cheerfully accepting more responsibility. It's normal that you have a share of the chores and are required to meet certain standards set by your parents. If your home is healthy, the more you contribute to a good family climate, the more freedom you will be given.

Parents who can't trust their children to fulfill small responsibilities won't trust them with large ones. But if you are trustworthy, helpful, and cooperative, they'll say yes to your requests for more latitude.

My parents are indifferent about issues that affect our society. How can I get them involved?

It's a very worthwhile thing to be interested in the larger issues of our society. By being involved and by sharing your enthusiasm with your parents, you may get them interested, too.

If you cheerfully ask their opinion about some of these issues and don't get upset when they say "I don't know anything about that" or "Why are you interested in that?" you may really awaken them.

I have known apolitical parents who, when their son decided to be a conscientious objector during the war in Vietnam, gradually discovered it was a true issue and ended up taking sides in that great national debate. I've seen people get interested in other issues when their children got involved first.

But, again, it is a mistake to think you have the power to change anybody. If you think that, you are setting yourself up for consistent disappointment. All you can do is change yourself and hope your example or your actions will help others change.

What do you say to your parents when you know you're wrong and you don't want to get yelled at?

One of the most marvelous things we can learn is to say, "Yes, you're right, I was wrong about that, and I apologize."

People find that very disarming. And you're relieved of the enormous burden too many people carry: that of having to defend things they know are wrong.

Unfortunately, your parents may yell when you say,

"Yes, I made a mistake and I'm sorry about it." Let them. But remember, it doesn't mean they hate you. Underlying their explosion is disappointment and frustration.

Now you can say, "Well, I said I was sorry and that I was wrong." Naturally, some parents will lecture at such a time. If yours do, let them express themselves. You have already deflated the balloon and minimized the damage caused by your mistake. Given that you've accepted it as an error in judgment, you can go on and learn from it. All of us make mistakes. To admit them and learn from them is the path to maturity.

What do you do when your parents believe an adult before you?

Pick a neutral time, when you're not all excited about a particular issue, and say, "You believed that person rather than me. I find that very hurtful; it's as if you don't trust me or my word. Could you explain why that's so? Why don't you choose to believe me?"

Parents who, for whatever reason, always side with other adults against their children make a terrible mistake. This is a particular problem with sexual molestation and other forms of child abuse. When adults commit crimes against small children in our society, some parents don't believe their children, and the crimes are allowed to continue.

Adults should pay attention to children and trust their word, unless they've already proven untrustworthy.

I feel that my parents don't communicate well with each other, and that leads to them not communicating with their kids well. How does a teenager go about changing this?

Understand, first, that you cannot hope other people will change because of your efforts. The moment you accept that, life becomes easier.

Let them know independently that you love each of them. That's your task: to love each of them.

Being aware that they seem to be having marital problems and that you're a victim of that, you don't have to choose sides or get involved in their dispute. Rather, be as affirming and as cheerful an influence as you can.

Usually, if you search, you'll find programs like Marriage Encounter or Marriage Enrichment, or sessions on parent-child relationships at your school or church. Sometimes they're sponsored by parents' clubs. If you have influence with your parents, perhaps you can get some literature about the program and hand it to them and say, "I really think you ought to go to this."

Not uncommonly, I have spoken at such a gathering, and parents have come up and said "I was ready to go to bed, but my daughter said she was ready to disown me if I didn't come to this" or "It's because of our son we're here this evening. He heard you this morning at the student assembly, and insisted we be here."

Nudge your mother or father, perhaps, by saying, "You and Mom don't appear very happy. How come you don't seek marriage counseling?"

It's the best thing you can do—if you do it in a loving fashion.

What would you suggest for a person whose mother wants to be a friend but, when arguments come up, starts saying "But I'm the mother!"?

At present you're going through a period of sorting out your life and deciding where you're headed, who you are, and how you relate to the people around you. Meanwhile, your mother is trying to move to a new level of relating to you, as a friend. That's one of the tasks of adolescents and parents, to move from the relationship of child to parent to one of equals.

Gradually, until you're twenty or twenty-two, your relationship will keep moving toward friendship. But until then, as long as you're remaining at home, there'll come times of tension and moments when your mother must assert parental authority and no longer be your friend.

What I mean is this: Friendship occurs among people who can treat one another as equals. But the moment one person has to lay down the law—which is your mother's responsibility—there is inequality.

As long as you are living at home and are under her jurisdiction, your mother has that authority. That kind of flip-flopping from equality to inequality will occur for a while, but it should disappear by the time you're on your own. You can help it along by paying attention to my earlier comments about not arguing but instead discussing.

How do I tell my dad that I don't like the way he treats me?

Sometime when you're not in conflict with him, say, "You know that last argument we had, I really think we both could have handled it better. I think you'd get a lot further with me if you'd talk to me quietly instead of shouting and storming and also if you'd let me give my side." Whatever the issue is, address it that way.

You might try discussing issues you're reading about in this book. Many parents have had no training in parenting except from their own parents, and they're probably doing a better job than their parents did with them. If you're his first adolescent, you are a whole new territory for him, and he's got to learn on the job.

You can give clues on how he might deal with you more effectively. Sometime when you are at peace with one another, speak openly about how you'd prefer him to handle certain issues. Tell him how you're willing to cooperate in the mutual task of building friendship between you.

What happens if your parents don't like your boyfriend? How do you persuade them he's OK?

Invite him home for dinner. Tell your parents, "You know, I really want you to get to know him. I don't want to have to skulk around corners with him; I'd like you to meet him." Perhaps they haven't had a chance to find out he's a nice person and not a threat to your well-being.

Also, if you feel romantically involved, and especially if you feel sexually attracted, try to listen to what your friends and family say about your boyfriend.

In adolescence, people sometimes choose a "love object" and project upon this object the idea that he or she is perfect, wonderful, and will answer all one's dreams. They turn even vices into virtues. She may be sloppy and irresponsible, and a boy will say, "Oh, she's so carefree." He may be unkempt and smell bad, and she'll say, "Oh, he's so masculine."

A marriage based on that kind of infatuation will be in deep trouble.

One way to find out whether you really love this boy is to see you do not get impatient or upset with the objections of your friends and family when they say, "I don't think he's good for you." Listen to their reasons, and see the boy through their eyes for a while. That helps you get an objective handle on the emotional state of mind you're in. Do their objections fit?

It would've saved a great deal of suffering by a few million girls last year if they had listened to what other people had tried to tell them.

Another test is to ask yourself how your relationship has

affected you: Have your parents complimented you on how much energy and cooperation you've shown at home? Have your teachers complimented you on your new cheerfulness? Have your grades improved? If not, the relationship is harming you and therefore is not loving.

Try those tests first. Then ask your parents if you can invite your friend home to meet them. That might change their attitude.

5

Making My Own Decisions

5

What do you do if parents pressure you to be something you don't want to be? They want me to be an all-American, Boy Scout, pre-med type, but I'm just not like that. Maybe I want to be a drummer in a rock band, or even a motorcycle racer. Why can't I choose for myself? We're having a lot of arguments about this.

If your parents are encouraging you to pursue academic excellence, they're right. Your most important task—aside from helping create a healthy family at home—is to learn all you can about yourself and life in general. Your schoolwork helps you learn about the world of ideas, history, literature, and the arts. Those things help make life worthwhile.

But if your parents are setting specific career guidelines for you, ordering you to be a premed student and go to medical school, they are making a grave mistake. You have a right to be your own person and follow your own destiny.

Some parents want their sons or daughters to fulfill dreams they didn't accomplish for themselves. Others want their kids to follow precisely in their own footsteps.

At your age, you should have a chance to look at all the possibilities. That includes both your own dreams and the ones your parents have for you. Where do you want to be ten years from now? What do you want to be doing? What income level do you wish to have? How do you go about achieving those goals? What are you doing today to lay the foundations for who, where, and what you want to be ten years from now?

When the time comes to make these decisions, then you can go to your parents and—if you so choose—say, "I'm sorry, I do not intend to go to medical school."

I want to commit myself to my girlfriend, but my parents think that high school students should devote more time to friends instead. What do you think?

I agree with your parents. In high school you should be going to dances, movies, shows, and picnics with a number of people of the opposite sex (preferably in groups, which will keep you from feeling heavy sexual pressure).

It is a drastic mistake to tie yourself to one person too early, thus limiting your social encounters. Teens who latch on prematurely to a boyfriend or girlfriend often make disastrous marriage choices. Others later begin wondering about the people they never got to meet, the friendships they never had, the exciting opportunities and people they missed.

And premature commitment to a boyfriend or girlfriend often leads to premature sex. That in turn often leads to disillusionment, pregnancy, or premature marriage. Those are all terrible blows to your self-esteem.

If you want a happier future, you'll spread your friendship among many people and not limit yourself now.

What happens if your parents are not giving you encouragement in the things you do (especially going to church and church-related things)?

It's too bad your parents aren't encouraging you. Perhaps they are discouraged themselves, for one reason or another, and don't know what to make of the spiritual dimension of life.

That is no reason for you to be discouraged about your activities. In adolescence you are defining who you are under

God. It is a time to explore the spiritual. Indeed, a number of young people would be living much happier lives if they did not neglect the spiritual side of their lives.

Perhaps you could invite your parents to church. They may find a world they didn't know existed. One thirteen-year-old girl I know started going to church and soon came home and said, "Why don't we say grace at meals?" Before long the family was saying grace at meals. Then she said, "I'd really like you to come to church with me." Within a year her parents were members of her church.

Children can influence their parents with their lifestyle and example—and invitations.

At what age has a person reached full maturity and the ability to handle adult responsibilities?

Some of my clients are fifty years old but still asking "Who am I, what do I want to do with my life?" and thinking of leaving their spouses and children in order to answer adolescent questions like these. I know sixteen-year-old kids who are more responsible and mature than they are.

Maturity is not a matter of chronological age. There is no point at which you are suddenly grown up. I'm fifty-six and still growing. I expect to keep on growing.

When you accept responsibility for your actions, cooperate with others, do your best to fulfill commitments, encourage others to do their best and give them credit when they do, then you are being mature, whether you are sixteen or fifty-six.

I don't know what to do when I graduate. I am scared of the future. My parents always hassle me.

Everyone faces this plight sometime in life. You are at a major point of transition, and you must make a number of decisions. Do you want to go to college? Move away from home? Get a job? What track are you getting onto? What kind of occupation do you want?

Remember, if you need to, you can unmake or remake these decisions later. They're not eternal.

Being "scared" is normal. Whenever we move from an area to which we're accustomed into a new area strange to us, it is scary. Don't forget, though, that another word we have for scary is "exciting." Scary things are challenging. And new. And exhilarating. Facing scary things is an adventure.

You are about to start an exciting adventure in life, and, yes, it will be scary. But it'll be scary when you graduate from college, or when you move away from home. It'll be scary when you decide to marry, and when your first baby is due. It'll be scary when you take on a mortgage. Scariness is part of a fully lived life.

When you say your parents "hassle" you, perhaps you mean that because you're scared, almost any approach seems irritating. Your parents may simply be trying to learn what your plans are, but because you don't know yourself, you feel threatened by their questions.

The best way to stop that is by sharing your concerns and confusions with them. If you say, "Here's where I am, and here are the options I confront, and I've been thinking of doing this one. What do you think?" then, instead of hassling you, they'll be helping you plan the future.

Whether we think somebody is hassling us or helping us often depends on how we feel. If your parents are simply saying, "What are your plans, and have you looked at what it is you want to do for the future?" they're trying to get you to open up with them.

Your parents are assets. As you graduate from high school and become more firmly established as an adult, try to treat your parents as equals and let them know what's going on inside you. In other words, allow them that new dimension of parenting. That may seem scary, too, but if you can manage it, you'll find they can be a big help to you.

Isn't it unfair for parents who are from another country with a totally different culture to try and bring kids up the same way they were brought up, when the kids want to go by the American way because it is their society?

That clash of cultures is not uncommon. We have many new immigrants from Asia, Latin America, and elsewhere. Your parents are in a new culture and may feel very threatened because they may not have learned the standards of their new country.

You can bridge the old world and the new. You've planted your feet firmly in the new world, among new friends, and you are adapting. Be patient with your parents, who are doing the best they know how. They're scared and clinging to what is familiar. You don't want to engage in warfare with them, you want to be their educator. You want to be able to say, "That was OK in your country, but in this country it's done this way, and we are citizens of this country now."

Remember, they've had a lifetime of learning a different way of being a parent. And now they're in a strange world, cut off from their roots and from the support they had there. If you fight them, you'll isolate them even further and make them even more scared and unhappy.

Also, you should value your family's ethnic heritage. It would be a shame if you forget the language of your ancestors. We need as many multilingual people as we can get in this society; they are valuable culturally, socially, and professionally. Share ethnic celebrations with your family. Be proud of your heritage.

Still, you don't have to be an oddball at school. You have the right to fit in to your new culture. If you can, take a positive approach and try to help your parents adapt to their new life.

What do you do with parents who constantly want to know where you are, whose house you're at, what their phone numbers are, when you view it as an invasion of your personal privacy?

How would you like your parents to leave early one morning without telling you, not return until late at night —and not leave word how to reach them in an emergency?

Probably not much, because we assume family members will keep one another posted about where they will be. In my city of San Francisco we're aware an earthquake could happen at any time. Emergencies can happen anywhere. So, whether I go out for an evening or for a cross-country trip, my teenagers at home know my itinerary, flight plans, and telephone numbers.

Your family has the same obligations. If your mother or father were asked where you were, when you were due home, and how you could be reached in an emergency and could only answer "I don't know," we would accuse them of being irresponsible parents.

Your parents care about you and care about your welfare; therefore, they also care to know your whereabouts. It's their responsibility to know and yours to let them know. That's one of the things that makes for well-functioning families.

Why is it so improper for teens to spend their own money on their own things, such as BMX bikes and record albums? My parents always object, even though they themselves spend money on unnecessary things, like magazines, beer, and cigarettes.

I can't legislate for your parents. All I can say is, in my family, kids who had their own money, whether it came from Christmas gifts or from part-time work, could spend or save it as they wished.

Of course, when other factors are involved—are your parents worried about your safety on a BMX bike?—then your parents have a right to be concerned and should be involved in your decision.

But when it comes down to spending your money on records, a concert, clothes, makeup, or the like, you have a right to make the choices. That's how you will learn to responsibly handle your financial assets in the future—by handling your financial assets now.

Your decisions may be wrong, but you'll discover that for yourself soon enough. In a few weeks the thing you bought may fall apart, or the record may just gather dust. Or you won't be able to go somewhere or do something because you have spent all your money on other things. That's part of your education too.

Perhaps you should show your parents this answer.

Right now I don't want to have to talk to my parents about my problems, but they want me to tell them what's going on. I feel as if they are just kind of there. I don't want them to bother me: I just want to do what I want to do. I don't want to feel that way, but how do I change my feelings?

You probably are working through—on a rather deep level—some of the major questions I've discussed throughout this book: who you are, what you want to do with your life, where you are going. You're trying to think things through. You need this time free of distractions.

But your parents may think you have withdrawn too far from them, and they may be worried. Possibly they want to try to help you, stay in touch with you. You then become angry because they're moving into your space.

Probably the best thing is for you to make a very clear statement to them. Say "Right now I'm a bit confused" or "Right now I need my privacy" or "Right now I'm just mulling things over awhile; don't worry, I still love you and I'll stay in touch with you, and I'm not going to do anything dumb."

You have a right to your privacy. But when you feel the need to withdraw into yourself and mull things over, try to maintain some connection with your parents. They may have been reading articles and hearing warnings from people like me that, when children withdraw too far, it can be a sign of drug abuse or suicidal depression.

Therefore your parents might be very concerned, and be doing their best to be loving, responsible parents, in trying to find out what's going on with you.

Reassure them you're OK, in a way that shows you love them and that you're not going to do anything stupid. If you can do that, you'll help raise their consciousness of who you are, and you'll probably find they'll respect that.

How do you explain to your parents that you aren't going to make the same mistakes your brothers and sisters did; you'd like to make your own mistakes?

Parents who've had a son or daughter involved with teenage pregnancy or a drunk driving accident tend to be overcautious with the younger kids in the family. It's a natural response. They're terrified of those mistakes. They may also blame themselves and feel very guilty. It will help if you understand that.

Of course, *you* aren't your older brother or older sister. You aren't the one they're worried about. So reassure them by saying it quite openly: "I'm not so-and-so, I'm me. And I may make some mistakes, but I won't make the mistakes they made. I've seen what happens, and I don't plan to have it happen to me." See how they respond.

Let them know you need to assume more responsibility for yourself. Give them reassurance and love, realizing all the while it is as inevitable as tomorrow morning's sunrise that you'll have your freedom soon anyway.

Why do parents question my decisions?

The better question is, Why are you so defensive? If you find yourself explaining and justifying, it means you're probably unsure about your decision, too.

Are your parents asking simple Why did you do this? or Why did you do that? questions? Those are dumb questions, I agree. I've never know anybody to go out and say, "I'm going to do this dumb thing for a dumb reason." Most people go out and do this dumb thing for a good reason.

On the other hand, some parents tend to oversupervise, and, unfortunately, it creates resentment and tempts kids to try increasingly irresponsible actions in an attempt to say, "I'm my own person."

It could also be that your parents are testing you to see if you've thought your decisions through.

These are only some of the reasons your parents may be questioning your decisions.

Try discussing things with your parents before you make a decision. Let them help you arrive at a conclusion that is mature and thoughtful. That way they probably won't question the decision afterward.

What if you are afraid to try that reasonable approach? Perhaps you fear their questions will shine too bright a light upon your decision. And if you become defensive and evasive, perhaps you should stop and wonder if your decision really is the right one after all.

Is TV supposed to be taken away from us if the show is not approved by our parents?

Not all things on television are suitable for all people, and some things aren't suitable for anybody.

As I pointed out earlier, the influence of television is enormous; by the time you graduate from high school you will have had eleven-thousand hours of classroom instruction and over twenty-thousand hours of television.

Anything you put in your head stays there, particularly the extremely powerful images of television. In those twenty-thousand hours of television you'll have seen a third of a million commercials, most of them in behalf of heavily sugared edibles. You will have seen countless murders and assaults and thousands of immoral sexual encounters.

Ask yourself: is that what you want put in your head? And aren't your parents right to ask the same question in your behalf?

In my family we controlled the television set. When my children grew older, we controlled it by watching programs together. When the car commercial came on, I could ask, "What does that semi-nude woman have to do with the performance of that automobile?" During a show I could ask, "Why did the director move in for a close-up of that person at this time?" That way I could teach my children how these images from television are used to manipulate us.

I could teach them a bit of television appreciation and help them develop a faculty for watching critically. (I think education beats censorship any day.)

Every minute you use is a portion of your life's time. Ask yourself if watching this commercial for cola, or that bit of dramatized adultery, is a proper way to be spending your life. Do you really want to spend your life putting that inside your skull?

I suspect you have responsible parents if they are supervising your television watching.

Why do parents make such a big fuss about teenagers seeing R-rated movies? Do they think we're going to do everything we see on the movie screen? They say it influences us because we are still setting our values. I feel people are still setting values no matter what age they are. They know what's right from wrong in R-rated movies, and I feel I know right from wrong as well. So why should they be able to see these movies when we can't?

You pose a good question. Why do your parents feel they can handle R-rated material better than you can? For one thing, they have greater experience. That means they can distinguish fact from fantasy a bit better than you probably can. It's an interesting topic to discuss with them.

If your parents are going to such a film, that's a time to say, "Can I go along? I think I can handle it. And if you don't think I can handle it, you can quiz me afterward." I think that's a perfectly appropriate thing to say.

When something objectionable happens on television, I don't jump up and shut off the screen. Censorship like that doesn't work very well. Instead, I ask my kids, "Why do you think that happened? And what do you feel about that? How do you believe that affected the people involved? What are your feelings about that?" We've usually found it a great learning experience to discuss such issues. As I said in the previous answer, I think education has it all over censorship in such matters.

According to one survey, 92 percent of the sexual relationships on television are immoral or illegal. The "R" rating means a film is for "mature audiences." Some "R" movies are excellent—but because of vulgar language, violence, or sexually explicit scenes are deemed unsuitable for young people. Your parents have a legitimate concern to protect you from that. But you *may* be mature enough to see some of these things with your parents, (which is what the "R" rating requires) and talk it over with them afterward.

Walt Whitman wrote, "There was a child who went forth every day, and the first object he looked upon, that object he became; and that object became part of him, for the day, or for a certain part of the day, or for many years, or stretching cycles of years."

The truth behind Whitman's statement is why there is a rating system and why responsible parents pay attention to the ratings.

My parents swear that rock music and music videos are the work of the Devil. But I know they are just being misinterpreted by my parents. Why can't they let me listen to what I want?

You may have a healthy approach to rock music, and your parents may be overreacting.

But you must admit that a lot of rock music does carry violent, death-wish messages and a good deal of throbbing sexuality that has very little to do with the real world. Such music can be, in a way, a drug.

Don't worry too much about your parents' overreaction; you're not going to convert them. I would advise you to take the rock music in small doses and remember there's a lot more to enjoy in life.

How do you talk to your parents about things they consider dangerous but that you want to do, such as joining a cult, or going hang gliding. Please assume I am an intelligent, reasonable person who is not easily fooled.

An intelligent, reasonable person does not join a cult. Cults require followers to give up their intelligence and reason. Such people tend to want somebody or some organization to tell them what to do, where to go, what to believe.

It's obvious your parents are fearful for your life. They're fearful for your spiritual and psychological life if you join a cult, and they're fearful for your physical life if you go hang gliding.

I think your parents have a right to say that as long as you live at home you shouldn't go around scaring them. And your answer should be, "OK, I won't."

Why do parents always tell us to clean our rooms? I like it messy. Don't I have a right to have my room the way I want it?

Yes. If it's your private room, you have a right to have it the way you want. One of my daughters put it this way: she knew it was time to clean her room when she couldn't find the bed.

Some parents waste a lot of energy fighting about a youngster's room, but it's an exercise in futility. An adolescent's room resembles the interior of his or her brain: one day neat and orderly, the next a total jumble.

Parents shouldn't expect that a teenager can keep a bedroom in perfect order when everything else in his or her life, desires, moods, and thoughts is disordered.

Your parents are seeking to instill a sense of order, harmony, and cleanliness in you. That's admirable, but maybe too much to expect from a teenager.

When parents come to me and ask, "How do I get John or Jane to clean the room?" my answer is, "You don't. Just keep the door closed. As long as strange smells do not emanate from the room, bubonic plague-bearing rats do not cascade from it, and it's not a fire or safety hazard, don't start any hassles about the room." Of course, we may draw the line at painting it black—but it is, ideally, your private space.

Not squabbling about teenagers' rooms saves a lot of energy on both sides.

Should your parents be able to tell you how to dress and who your friends should be? My mom says she'll ground me if I dress the way I want to, and I think that's really stupid. Also, do they have the right to tell you what kind of music to listen to? My mom threatens to burn my tapes if I don't stop playing them.

If you are dressing and selecting music in a fashion that is truly bizarre, your mother is right to be concerned.

Some teenage girls, experimenting with far-out dress, don't realize the impression they leave with the young men and young women around them, not to mention adults.

Perhaps when your mother was in high school, girls who dressed in a certain way were considered sexually available.

You may be emulating performers in their dress as a short-term fad, but your mother worries because she knows that often you're treated the way you're perceived, and suggestive dress can lead some people to assume the wrong things about you. Unfortunately, a bad reputation can help push you the wrong way in life.

You should try to sit down and discuss these issues with your mother. You have a right to try to reason with her. It always helps if you can learn her motivations, because then you know—and can discuss—precisely what she is worried about.

Another thing you can do is to save your money and get a pair of earphones. That way your mother won't hear your music unless she wants to. If you already use earphones, she may be concerned that you're using tapes to block out communication with the rest of the family. Don't make that mistake.

Do you think a parent whose child has always obeyed the rules and been good should trust this child at an unchaperoned party?

The lack of a chaperon always implies that you're going to do things you couldn't if an adult was around—meaning, usually, drinking, taking drugs, or having sex. That's what your parent is concerned about.

If the party is innocent, just a group of kids getting together for a good time, some dancing and music, why is it unchaperoned?

A lot of the disasters that strike teenagers—drunk-driving deaths, rapes of girls at parties, drug overdose deaths—have occurred at or after unchaperoned parties.

Your parent's concern is justified. Whether you can be trusted to go is not the question. Your parent must know and trust the other kids at the party, know how late the party will go on, whether there will be drinking at the party, and so on, before making a decision.

Do you think parents should buy the insurance and the car?

Nope. It deprives you of some of your first major adult decisions—earning the money to buy the vehicle and meeting the responsibilities for its upkeep.

Why is eighteen considered a magical year for adulthood? I'm fifteen and very responsible—even my parents say so. Why can't I have the freedom of an eighteen-year-old?

In most states, eighteen is the age at which you can begin to draw up contracts, go into debt, commit matrimony without your parents' consent, and do other adult things. At fifteen, you can't legally do these things, even though you may be more mature than some of the fifty-year-old clients I mentioned earlier.

Eighteen (and in some states, twenty-one) is an age picked arbitrarily, no matter how mature or immature you may be. The arbitrariness of that may rankle you, but imagine the alternative: yearly intelligence and maturity tests to see if you are eligible to sign contracts, drink, or vote.

It's a fact of life. Be patient; three years from now you may wish you didn't have to face some of these "freedoms" and the responsibilities they entail.

Why do parents think that you still have to go to bed at nine as you did when you were younger, rather than later, when you get tired?

Young children need the security of a set bedtime and routine. But as you grow older you have homework to do and social activities in which to take part. Your bedtime should indeed become more flexible.

By the time you've reached sixteen or seventeen, for example, your bedtime should be your own business. If you're still up reading or writing a letter, your parents shouldn't hassle you. I don't think you should be watching TV at midnight on a school night, but, in your own room, when you choose to go to sleep is your business.

What should you do if your parents always complain that you don't do enough work around the house, but you think you do more than enough?

What do you think is enough? For some people, taking a sack of garbage out to the trash can might seem an immense chore. Others willingly go on to weed the garden, fix the back fence, do the dishes. You need to clarify what your parents expect of you and what you feel able to do.

Sit your parents down and together work out a written list of things you do or need to do. Nail it down: what do you have to do on Monday, Tuesday, Wednesday, Thursday, Friday, and so on.

Once you've agreed upon a list, stick to it, and the complaints should stop.

What do you do when your parents don't like your friends?

Bring them home one at a time so your parents can get to know them. The unknown is always more scary than the known; your parents may frown on your friends because they don't know them.

Peer pressure often seems the enemy of parents. That's why some parents react suspiciously when you are close to kids they don't know.

So you should say, "Mom, is it all right if I bring Jerry home for dinner?" If your mother answers, "Well, I don't care for him," you can say, "You don't know him, really, and I'd really like to have him over to dinner." If Jerry really is such a great person, your mom and dad may take a liking to him.

But if Jerry doesn't want to come over to your house for dinner, you might ask yourself what kind of friend he is and why he is uncomfortable with a normal family. In that case your parents may be right about him.

What could I do to convince my father to let me go to my favorite group's concert (a group he doesn't like)?

Pluck a few reviews on the group's work from newspapers or magazines, and show them to your father. Ask him to listen to a few of the songs you think are particularly good. Perhaps you could even say, "How about going with me, Dad?" That might be a major breakthrough for you and not so outlandish as you might think. After all, many of the best rock stars are in their forties these days.

How come I'm old enough to know right from wrong but not old enough to do certain things?

Knowing right from wrong and being able to control your impulses are two very different things.

There isn't a person on this continent who doesn't know alcoholism is bad. So why are there millions of alcoholics in the United States?

There isn't a person who doesn't know that drugs can harm you physically, emotionally, and psychologically. So why do so many stars, athletes, and young people die from drugs every year?

Everyone knows cigarettes are wrong for his or her body (deadly, in fact). So why do millions of people still smoke, and why do many young people start the habit?

Most people know it's not a good thing to give birth to a baby when you don't have money, a family, or a marriage to support the life of the child. So why do a million girls, some as young as twelve, get pregnant every year?

These people knew these things were wrong, but they did them anyway. They were in social or personal situations that were beyond their control. They were with people who said that, though these things are wrong, they are still OK.

They were in a social environment that said what is wrong is right.

That's why your parents won't let you do certain things even though you know right from wrong.

Should a teen be made to go with his family on vacation when he may have other options with friends and school?

If your family is like most, you're all shooting off in different directions. Your sisters may have jobs or school activities to go to, you may have a job or football practice, and your parents have social and professional obligations. It's very difficult to keep your family together in one place doing the same thing—and enjoying life—all at the same time.

A vacation is a time of family bonding. You're all devoting prime time to having a good time together as a family. Vacation is another word for recreation: the re-creation of family ties, of intimacy, of bonding through fun and time together. Why do you want to avoid this chance to be with your family?

At your age it may be hard to believe, but fathers and mothers die and brothers and sisters move across the country. Believe me, your family will not always be with you.

Create some good memories of your family vacations— now. You'll have plenty of time to be with your friends during the rest of the year and the rest of your life.

6

Divorce and Separation

6

My dad died suddenly a couple of years ago. Now my mom's boyfriend usually stays over Friday or Saturday nights—in her bedroom. I hate it. Do I have a right to ask Mom to stop having him over so much?

It's unwise for your mother to entertain her boyfriend in her bedroom with you at home. You are still grieving for your father, and this situation is very distressing to you.

You should discuss this openly with your mother. You have a right to feel the way you do, and a right to tell her. She might not know how you feel.

It would help if you understand your mother's feelings, too. She may be considering marriage again, and she has a right to be married again if that's what she wants.

After my mother died of cancer, Dad became very aloof and distant. It's as though he can't get close to anyone anymore. My sisters and I feel very alone and frightened. What can we do?

Grief has made your father withdraw. If this has gone on for a long while, you are right to be concerned. It is a matter of serious concern.

First, read a paperback titled *How to Survive the Loss of a Love,* by Colgrove and McWilliams. Then give it to your father.

You might also try Bozarth-Campbell's *Life Is Hello, Life Is Goodbye* and Harold Kushner's *When Bad Things Happen to Good People.* These will help you both deal with the pain of losing your mother.

Second, try to make it clear to your father that your late mother would not appreciate his neglecting you and the rest of your family. It is no testimonial to her to prolong his grieving to the detriment of the family. She would want your family to regroup and grow closer, not more distant. You and your sisters should express both your love and your fears to him.

Third, if your father's withdrawal and grieving continues too much longer, talk to your family doctor about it. Your father's depression may require medical attention. An aunt, uncle, grandparent, teacher at school may be able to offer you help with this.

When my wife died suddenly a few years ago, my family grew much closer. Before, when I wanted my children to know something, or they wanted me to know something, it was often passed through their mother. Now suddenly we had to deal directly on every issue. We were pulled closer together in our pain, and we were able to express our love for one another much more openly.

Age makes no difference when you've lost somebody you love. You and your father have so much in common, it is important you try to help your father deal with his grief, and yours. Invite him to go with you and your sisters to a therapist so that you can all better cope with your loss.

My parents have been fighting a lot. I get very scared. What can I do?

Stay out of the fights, don't take sides, and wait until they've calmed down. Then go up to your mother or father —or both—and tell them that when they fight it scares you very much. Ask them to seek marital counseling. There's not much else you can do.

My parents are divorcing. How can I decide who to live with?

Remember that the choice is not which you love; you love them both. Nor which loves you; they both love you. The choice comes down to practical matters like which parent is closer to your school, which is more capable of dealing with you on a regular basis, which can take care of you from day to day.

In many states your parents can share custody, and you can spend an equal amount of time at each parent's home, providing they don't live too far apart.

Even if such an arrangement does not work for you, it is important you understand your mother and father are divorcing each other, not you. Your father will always be your father, and your mother will always be your mother.

They are still related to you in a bond of love, so try to make as loving a decision as you can.

When my parents divorced, they said it was for our good. If that's so, why did my dad move all the way up to Alaska and I never see him anymore?

When your parents said divorcing was for your good, they probably meant they were miserable and didn't want to continue inflicting their misery upon you.

Your father may have moved to Alaska for a well-paid job. He may have needed the money; a divorce can ravage family finances.

It's possible he moved because being in the same city or state was still miserable for him and your mother.

More important than why is what you can do to keep in touch with him. Write him letters. Once in a while, perhaps, you can call him on the phone. It may cost you ten or fifteen dollars, but you'll be able to chat with him for a few minutes and remind him you love him and you're still here.

When I come back from a visit with my dad, my mom always wants to know what he's doing, how much money he has, who he has for a girlfriend. It makes me very uncomfortable. How can I handle this?

To each question, respond, "You'll have to ask him." That must be your firm answer. You don't want to be a spy.

You can add, if you want, "Mom, I really think those are inappropriate questions, and I wouldn't answer them if Dad asked them about you, either."

You must be strictly impartial and not allow yourself to be made a messenger or spy; otherwise you'll be caught in the middle, and that will make you extremely uncomfortable.

From now on refuse to answer those questions. Perhaps you will raise your mother to a new level of self-awareness.

I hate my father for leaving my mom for another woman. Mom says I shouldn't, but I do. I never want to see him again. Is that so wrong?

You have every right to be angry with your father and to feel betrayed by him. You have a right to your feelings. Your mother's saying you shouldn't feel that way is missing the point. You feel the way you feel; it's not a matter of shoulds or shouldn'ts.

What you do about those feelings is another matter. You can do creative things with your feelings rather than destructive ones. You can decide not to let your feelings be destructive toward you, your mother, or your father.

Feelings don't last. Emotions are energy in motion. Feelings flow constantly, and if you're creative with them, you'll allow them to shift and change. Do not lock yourself into one set of feelings and imprison yourself in that way.

Your feelings are legitimate and honest—even normal— for someone in your situation. Later, though, you'll proba-

bly want to reestablish ties to your father. You may decide
he did the best he knew how, that he is human like the rest
of us. He didn't necessarily stop loving you, although he
ceased wanting to be married to your mother.

With that understanding may come a change in your
feelings about your father. When that happens, you should
let yourself go with those more positive emotions, too.

*A divorce occurred in my family. Why is it so much harder to get along
with one parent than with the other?*

You may be angry at the parent who divorced the other,
and you're blaming one and not the other. Obviously you
have reasons; feelings don't just come from nowhere. But
they are also temporary, and you may feel better about your
parent later as you gain more information and understanding.

If you are referring to the way one parent treats you, it
could be he or she feels guilty around you because of the
divorce.

How do you deal with a spiteful stepparent?

Occasionally a stepparent is jealous of a child's place in
the heart of the natural parent. Sometimes a child will treat
the stepparent in a rejecting fashion and thus help set up a
"spiteful" relationship. You might want to see if either of
these are true in your case. That will give you an idea how
best to deal with it.

At some point you may want to take your mother or
father aside and ask, "How can I best deal with so-and-so,
especially when . . . How do you suggest I handle it?" Try
not to make your parent have to defend the stepparent; that
won't help.

Why are so many divorces happening?

Many people think marriage will solve their problems. They don't realize marriage is full of struggle, trial, and the work of creating love, of making a marriage. When they find this out, they divorce.

Others marry because of infatuation or sexual attraction alone.

As George Bernard Shaw once commented, "When two people are under the influence of the most violent, most insane, most delusive, and most transient of passions, they are required to swear that they will remain in that excited, abnormal, and exhausting condition continuously until death do them part."

Today those who marry in that state often divorce when the initial passion subsides.

Unfortunately, many people think love is a hole in the ground, "I fell in love last year, but I got over it," or a kind of flu virus, "I'm in love, I can't help myself."

Earlier I noted love is not really an emotion, because emotions come and go but love stays. Love is a decision, a commitment of the will. You might dislike someone, but still love that person. In fact, in marriage there may come times you dislike—but still love—your partner.

The younger a person marries, the likelier he or she is to divorce very soon. Even when divorce occurs later—even after twenty-five years of marriage—in most cases it happens to people who were married as teenagers.

In other words, even if they stuck it out twenty-five years, they did not begin their marriage with mature expectations.

One might admire the courage of those who clung to marriage because of religious ideals, or for the sake of the children, or because they vowed, "I'm not gonna be a quitter." But the fact remains they made a bad decision and suffered long because of it.

The reasons people divorce flow often from the reasons they got married. Teenagers should attend good marriage education programs in high school. When they start thinking they're in love, they'd better do some serious study of what they mean by "love." If they think they ought to get married, they'd better take a thoughtful look at what they think marriage might be. Those who make mature decisions about when and whom to marry are much less likely to divorce.

My parents are divorcing. Dad and his fifteen-year-old son live with Dad's girlfriend and her four children. His thirteen-year-old and twelve-year-old also want to be with Dad, who is easier and more permissive than Mom. But Mom and I think it's much better for them to live with us. Should we stand by quietly, waiting to pick up the pieces, or demand custody no matter how much they object?

You probably should just stand by and let them bear the consequences of their decision.

To fight for, and get, custody of teenage kids who don't want to be there will cause a lot of turmoil for them, for you, and for Dad. It's unnecessary.

For one thing, Dad's new wife is probably not going to appreciate having all the new kids to take care of suddenly. You may find that your siblings will want to be at home sooner than you expect. The grass is always greener on the other side, until you get there and discover it's Astroturf.

How can I stay out of the middle of my parent's messy divorce? How can I be nonjudgmental and love each one when one is not acting very lovable and the other holds me at arm's length?

If one is holding you at arm's length and the other is not very lovable, it's because they're wrapped up in their own problems. You can't help feeling the pain of their dissolution, but try to understand that the pain is probably even greater for them. They probably have a sense of failure and a sense of losing their dreams and hopes about their marriage. These feelings often accompany divorce.

Even though one parent is distant and the other not lovable, try to be as kind to each of them as you can be.

I think your questions shows real, loving maturity. My hunch is that given time, their anger, guilt, and pain will subside, and you'll find them becoming more aware of you.

7

Drugs and Booze

7

Why do so many parents drink?

First, let's clarify "drinking." When I talk about drinking in this chapter, I don't mean an occasional drink or a glass of wine with dinner.

Rather, I mean heavy use or drunkenness. And when I talk about drugs, I mean any use that is not prescribed by a doctor for treating an ailment.

Now, no matter why people say they drink heavily, there's only one reason anybody overindulges in drink or drugs: they are trying to escape the pain they feel at being who they are. They have low self-esteem. Drugs (alcohol being the most common addictive drug) are used as an escape.

But the escape hatch becomes a trap.

People who abuse alcohol and drugs become alienated from other people. Often they suffer social rejection or job loss or ruined relationships. They then have even less sense of self-worth and greater self-hate, so they turn to more boozing and drug use.

That's why anybody drinks. If your parents are drinking too much, that's why.

My father can't talk to me or relate to me when he's sober. Then he gets drunk and starts trying to hug me and be friends with me, and he says he loves me. But I hate it. His breath stinks, and he's not himself. When I tell him to leave me alone, he gets mad and starts shouting at me.

Sometimes he even tries to hit me or Mom. If he can't accept me when he's sober, why should I accept him when he's drunk?

Your father feels very inhibited when he's sober. Drinking allows him to let out not only his good feelings but his bad ones as well. That's not unusual among alcoholics.

You have a right not to submit to expressions of affection from a drunk. I'd advise you to go into Al-Anon, or a teen Al-Anon group called Alateen, to learn how to cope with an alcoholic. These groups can help you. Your experiences are not so unusual.

In the meantime, stay out of your father's way as much as possible when he's drunk.

I'm considering going to Al-Anon, but I'm scared about walking into a group of people I don't know, and how do I find a group like this?

Almost every city has an Alcoholics Anonymous, Al-Anon, or Alateen group listed in the telephone book.

Once you walk in you'll find everybody there in exactly the same situation as you. You don't have to say anything. You can just sit and listen until you feel at ease. These meetings are geared for strangers to walk into and feel comfortable. Nobody will accost you or try to get you to talk. People only go by their first names, sometimes even made-up names.

You could ask your mother to go with you. Both of you need help dealing with an alcoholic.

Both my parents are alcoholics, and my father beats me. How can I deal with this and help them at the same time?

There are agencies in most states that work to prevent child abuse. When your father beats you in his drunkenness, that is child abuse. You have to seek protection. The best way to help him and get you some protection is to talk to your school counselor, who should know what to do.

If your school counselor won't help, speak to an adult you trust, a principal or teacher. Most school officials know what to do when a youngster is being beaten by a drunken father. Don't quit until someone helps you. If you get beaten again, call the police immediately. Your father needs help; they will see he gets it.

To learn how to cope with parental alcoholism, do follow the advice given earlier. Go to Al-Anon.

My mom drinks once in a while, and occasionally she gets a little drunk. I know it's probably OK, but I get this sick, disgusted feeling, and I start being sarcastic about her drinking. Why do I react this way?

Because a drunk is disgusting. (That's one reason not to become one.)

Seek out Al-Anon or Alateen. Get into a group that discusses how you deal with an alcoholic parent. Check out books and pamphlets at your library or doctor's office. Living with an alcoholic can be hell on earth, especially for children, and 28 million of them in the United States are growing up with an alcoholic parent right now.

Al-Anon and Alateen are support groups with whom you can discuss this on a weekly or daily basis. You're not alone in the world. There are things you can do, responses you can make, that can help relieve your suffering.

The best way for you to help your family to survive your parent's alcoholism is to seek help for yourself.

How much does a person have to drink to be an alcoholic?

There are alcoholics who don't drink, others who lose control with only one drink, and still others who can drink a bottle of whisky and not show any apparent effects.

Alcoholism is not determined by the amount or frequency a person drinks, but by his or her dependency on alcohol. An alcoholic cannot go without a drink for very long, cannot face a depressing or upsetting situation without alcohol.

Alcohol addicts are everywhere, and many of them do not look like the drunks you see portrayed on movie screens.

If drugs and alcohol are so bad, why do so many adults use them? Especially educated, successful, happy adults?

People who have a craving for drugs or booze are unhappy. They're trying to fill an empty space inside them.

But they fail. That's obvious from their need to keep increasing the dosage. They get worse.

Why do people use drugs and alcohol? Many have false notions of what life is supposed to be. Some believe desires should be gratified instantly. Others think life is meant to be euphoric and free of any pain.

And some believe that if they only can accomplish a particular goal, make this much money, become a star, then at last they'll be happy. Some of them work hard, earn money, become famous. And then they discover they're the same person they were before.

"There must be something more than this!", they think. Somebody tells them, "This'll make you feel real good," and hands them a drug.

These people may be educated and successful, but they are not happy. Happy people don't need drugs. If you think they do, you've been looking at too many liquor advertisements. Obviously, they aren't going to show you the people who are in the drunk tanks or lying in the gutters of our cities.

If drinking and doing drugs are OK for parents, why are they wrong for teenagers? The parents don't seem any worse for it, so why do they tell us we shouldn't?

Drinking and taking drugs are not okay for parents, any more than for teenagers. If your parents are taking drugs or drinking to excess, then you have an obligation as well as a right to protest. You might say, "You're not being a very good parent when you overindulge in booze, and you are definitely not setting a very good example for me when you're using drugs."

Is it worse for kids to drink than for adults?

Alcohol abuse is a disastrous choice for anyone at any age. It simply has an added dimension of tragedy which the drinking starts in adolescence.

The major task of adolescence is to put yourself together, to come to know yourself as a whole person.

But when youngsters take alcohol or drugs, addling their thoughts with mind-altering substances, they disintegrate and fragment themselves.

They're pulling themselves apart instead of becoming whole, and that can have only unfortunate consequences for their future. They create more problems for themselves—at a time when they already have enough.

All the girls go to the "cool" guys; all the "cool" guys drink; therefore, I have to drink in order to get a girlfriend.

You sound like someone who knows how to reason. I wonder if you think all the girls are so shallow as to think that drinking is "cool." Surely there are some girls in your school who are more intelligent than that.

You want a girl who shares your ideals, and is, like yourself, able to withstand peer pressure, in other words, a girl who is a leader, not a follower, who, like you, is able to see the destructive consequences of alcohol and other drugs.

If you find someone like that, you've got a friend in tune with you. She'll be a lot more fun than a girl who makes you change for the worse in order to date her.

How can I explain to my parents that everyone my age drinks, and that it's hard to keep away from it?

Surprise! Three-fourths of the brightest high school students in this country have never had sexual intercourse. Ninety percent of these two thousand student leaders had never tried cocaine, PCP, or any other hallucinogenic drug, amphetamine or barbiturate. Eighty-three percent had never used marijuana. Twelve percent who had tried pot discontinued using it.

Thirty-four percent said they occasionally drink hard liquor and 32 percent sometimes had a beer. That leaves 34 percent who don't drink.*

Further, in a study titled "Mood of American Youth" prepared for the National Association of Secondary School Principals, a survey of representative youths from across America disclosed that these young people felt drugs and alcohol were the worst influences on young people today. The overwhelming majority (82.6 percent) agreed with their mothers about drugs and 75.6 percent agreed with their fathers about them.

So, not everyone your age drinks. Only the losers. Leaders are people who don't follow any herd, but know how to say "no."

---

*Figures are from the fourteenth annual survey of the two thousand student leaders listed in the 1983 edition of *Who's Who Among American High School Students* (Lake Forest, IL: Educational Communications, Inc., 1983). Reported by the Associated Press in the *San Francisco Chronicle* on November 1, 1983.

How come, just because I don't drink or do drugs, and I'm a good person, people don't like me?

A leader—and that includes someone who refuses to follow the crowd—is a challenge to followers.

Followers want you to be just like them, and when you're not, they'll try to put you down. When you're different from them, they feel it's a judgment on them. They feel it as a measurement of how far they may have fallen, or of how little they may have climbed.

So, followers may, indeed, act negatively toward you, but they're not necessarily the friends you want anyway.

Ask yourself: what are the important factors in life? You are trying to find out who you are in relation to other people, and one of the things you found out is you're not a follower who takes drugs and alcohol. And therefore followers are going to call you "straight" or "square"; they're not going to care much for you.

Well, that's like oil and water. They don't mix.

Be patient. The consequences of your decision—and theirs—will be very obvious in a few years. And you'll be the winner.

TV and people like you try to scare kids into thinking that if they do a drug or take a drink, their lives are instantly over. I've never noticed any negative effects. Why should I listen to you?

I find your denial that drugs or alcohol have affected you rather strange. After all, we're talking about drugs and substances that are mind-altering, aren't we?

Your denial is normal for a drug user, because denial is characteristic of alcoholics and substance abusers. The user is the last to admit he or she has a problem.

Until they stop denying, they can't be cured of the

problem that is causing them and so many other people pain.

If you're so put together, why do you need a drug or drink to feel good? Why do you depend on something from outside to feel good inside? You need to ask yourself this question. Why don't you feel good naturally? Most people do.

Why shouldn't we do drugs if we want to?

You can do anything you want. If you want to do drugs, you can; they're everywhere. If you want to get F's in school, you can. The real question is, Why would you want to do these things?

Always look at your motives. If you want to do something self-destructive, what does it say about you? Why do you want to injure yourself?

In one in-depth survey of one hundred teenage suicides, 71 percent had been involved with drugs or alcohol prior to their committing suicide.

Drugs and alcohol are a suicidal foreplay. They are little deaths. People try to kill themselves in little ways, to put themselves out of their misery.

Remember, emotions change. If you're feeling self-destructive today, you may not feel that way tomorrow. But if you become addicted now, it will affect the rest of your life.

I use a lot of marijuana and, sometimes, cocaine or angel dust. I feel guilty when I do it. I can't tell my parents. I don't want to go to my teachers. I don't have anyone to turn to. What should I do?

Drop into a branch of Narcotics Anonymous, which, like Alcoholics Anonymous, will preserve your confidentiality and help you kick a drug habit. Most major cities have narcotics treatment centers or hot lines, and they respect your confidentiality, too—so will your family doctor.

Parents can call the National Federation for Parents for Drug-Free Youth at 1-800-554-KIDS. You can call the American Council for Drug Education at 1-301-984-5700, and they will give you whatever help they can.

If you have a cocaine, or any drug problem you should call the Fair Oaks Hospital in Summit, New Jersey, at 1-800-COCAINE or 1-800-662-HELP for information.

How can I help a friend who is heavily into drugs but won't admit she has a problem?

As long as she denies her problem you can't do much. She is the only person who can seek help. But you can, at least, refuse to help her get drugs and refuse to cover up for her when she's using them.

I would also advise that you discuss this matter with your school counselor. Perhaps someone in authority can be of help to her before it is too late.

I'm seventeen. My parents won't let me drink, yet they tell me all the time that they drank when they were my age. It seems unfair.

I'm going to assume that you are saying they are citing their experience as a basis for their concern and their refusal to have you suffer as they did. Your parents know from experience that youthful drinking is not good for you. If they want to protect you from the ill consequences of alcohol, that's not unfair.

Do you think moderate alcohol use (I don't mean abuse) can actually help a family?

I have nothing against a beer at a barbecue, or wine with dinner, but I don't know how it can help a family. I've never known a doctor or psychiatrist who said, "I think your family should take up drinking."

How do you tell your parents to quit smoking?

If they're addicted to nicotine, telling them won't help. People quit only when they want to.

Most people realize they'd live about ten years longer if they gave up cigarettes today. I know a fifty-five-year-old man who stood chain-smoking outside the funeral home where his brother lay in a casket after dying from lung cancer. People stop only when they want to stop.

But you can, at least, benefit from their example. Don't start smoking; you can see how hard it is to quit.

What's the truth about smoking pot, as far as its effect on health?

Lung problems in smokers, chromosomal damage in smokers' children. Go to your public library and look up recent articles for yourself in the *Guide to Periodical Literature.*

What's wrong with chewing tobacco?

Kids who chew tobacco have developed cancer of the mouth, lip, and tongue, which are not pleasant to look at, let alone die from. It definitely limits your social life to people who are insensitive to bad tastes and odors.

If my dad does drink too much, what can I do about it?

The best thing you can do immediately is to get in touch with a local branch of Al-Anon. If you don't find it in the phone book, you'll surely find Alcoholics Anonymous. Call them and ask about an Al-Anon program for teenagers. In some areas it's known as Alateen.

You can't hope to change your father, but you can hope to change yourself so that you don't contribute to his alcoholism. Many children and spouses of alcoholics are "enablers." They unconsciously help the alcoholic hide his or her problems and keep drinking.

One of the best ways to deal with any problem of any kind is to find out where to go for help. In your case, Al-Anon is it.

8

The Blues

8

I think about suicide sometimes. There's absolutely no future for me. I can't succeed. I don't belong. I'm only seventeen, and already my life is worthless. I'm kind of afraid to tell anybody about my thoughts of suicide. I mentioned it lightly once to my mom, but it didn't help. What should I do?

Everyone under great stress—that includes teenagers and kids (as well as their parents)—thinks about suicide at some time or another. An immediate response when those thoughts or feelings are strong is to look in your phone book white pages for your local suicide prevention crisis line. Call them and talk. When you say there's no future for you and life is worthless, you are expressing a very profound depression. I urge you to get help for this right away.

That you mentioned it "lightly" to your mom was probably why she took it lightly. Talk seriously to her or go immediately to your counselor at school and ask him or her to refer you to a professional.

I know from my work with many suicidal adolescents and preadolescents that they can change their view of themselves. They can feel much happier about their lives. In fact, none of my clients has ever committed suicide.

Your feelings are caused by how you perceive yourself, how you perceive your future, how you perceive your life. Those perceptions can change.

Above all, you don't want to make a permanent decision based upon a temporary mood. No matter how long your mood seems to last, it is only temporary. It will pass away, and you want to be around when it does. At seventeen you have as much of a future as any other seventeen-year-old in the world.

You must overcome these feelings of low self-esteem, low self-worth, and low self-image. The best way to do that is with a therapist, as soon as possible.

My older brother was smart and successful, and everybody loved him. Recently he shot himself in the head. I don't know if my family can survive. Why did he do it? Why didn't anyone realize he might do this? How can we pick up the pieces?

Some people with low self-esteem work hard to achieve. They chase after awards and good grades, hoping that these will make them feel they are worthwhile. But that feeling cannot come only from outside things; it has to come from inside, too.

Such people appear smart and successful, but it's a mask. Inside they feel alienated and hollow. They feel like the person in the previous question.

One day on impulse they pull a trigger and blow away what could have been a beautiful life—if only they had sought therapy. Moreover, they not only destroy themselves but they also partly destroy the people they leave behind, as you so eloquently express. Their friends and family ask themselves "What could I have done?" and feel enormous guilt, grief, and depression.

That makes suicide an especially nasty thing to do. And that's why I entirely disapprove of high schools holding memorial services with tear-jerking eulogies for a boy who has killed himself.

Instead, the principal should gather the school together

and say, "So-and-so just behaved like a jerk. He played a nasty, dirty trick on himself and, worse, on all of us. He should have sought help." That would be a much better memorial service, because it might stop other kids from making the same mistake.

It might help you cope with your grief if you realize the success and happiness you saw in your brother, was a facade. Behind it were feelings of worthlessness, failure, and sorrow—and perhaps even a romance that soured, or secret drug use, or something else you know nothing about.

I urge your family, as a family, to seek grief counseling.

I think one of my friends might kill herself. What should I do about it?

You should immediately tell your counselor, your principal, and—if they can't help—your friend's parents. Take this seriously.

Recently, a group of high school boys were talking. One said, "I'm going to go home tonight and watch TV." Another said, "I'm going to go out to a movie." A third one said, "I'm going to go home and kill myself." The others thought he was joking. But he went home and blew his head off.

You must take such warnings seriously. It's much better to err on the side of preventing it than to keep this secret to yourself and watch your friend murder herself. You're not doing your friend a favor if you become an accessory to her suicide by not telling someone who can help. A human life is at risk.

Don't think you are ratting on your friend when you go for help. By telling you her thoughts, your friend is really crying "Help!" to you. She wants you to tell somebody because she's afraid to tell anyone herself.

Kids often don't feel they can talk to their parents about their unhappy feelings. But they have teachers who care about them, aunts and uncles, relatives, principals, and counselors in places like community mental health clinics. You can walk in and tell them. Call the suicide prevention crisis line and discuss the matter. They will listen. They're trained.

How do I deal with a father who has been diagnosed as a depressed person but refuses to acknowledge his problem?

First, contact the person who diagnosed him and ask what you can do.

Second, if your mother is still present, talk to her about your feelings. She can talk to him without you being in the direct line òf fire. That might help get him to seek the treatment, psychological and medical, which can raise him up out of his depression.

A depressed person is "toxic." Just being near such a person depresses everybody. Whenever you're in his vicinity, you're going to feel down. There's an energy flow between people; depressed people suck your energy.

So try to limit your time near this island, this cesspool of depression, and be as cheerful as you can.

Everyone gets "down" once in a while, right? How do you know when it's serious?

Everybody does get down from time to time; if you didn't, you wouldn't know what being up felt like. That's one of the wild and wonderful things about our emotional lives: we go up and down and sometimes sideways.

It's when you have no up that you should get help—not just sad, not just a little down, but a full-scale depression, when you feel hapless, helpless, and hopeless for days on end. It's much easier to deal with depression early rather than later.

If you have suicidal thoughts flit across your mind occasionally, like "I wish that I were dead sometimes," that's no big deal. But if you mull over how you would do it, actually believing it possible, then you must seek help immediately.

When I'm feeling really depressed, what can I do to snap myself out of it?

Try to figure out how you're depressing yourself. What depressing things are you telling yourself? How are you cutting yourself off from challenges; how are you cutting yourself off from excitement?

A mild depression, when you don't know where it comes from, often is caused by an area inside us that seems sort of dead but is demanding new life. If you've moved, you may be grieving for your old home. Or if your dog was killed a week ago, you're still grieving for it. It's useful to ask yourself, "How am I depressing myself? Where is this coming from?" In the cases mentioned you have a right to be sad for a while—you wouldn't be normal if you didn't have periods like that.

But when it is prolonged, ask yourself what you are doing to depress yourself, and try to deal with that. If your depression still continues, seek a mental health professional. Most of them are experienced in dealing with depressed people, and they can give you some pointers.

The book I mentioned earlier, *How to Survive the Loss of a Love,* can help with emotional loss.

Suicidally depressed teenagers often have constant headaches or stomachaches, or they develop other bodily problems, like rashes. These are symptomatic of their bottling up a lot of anger, resentment, or sadness, and all of that affects their bodies.

And as I mentioned in the prior chapter, 71 percent of the

kids who committed suicide had been involved with drugs or alcohol prior to killing themselves. So, obviously, it's important to stay away from drugs and alcohol. Alcohol is a depressent, and the drug induced "high" is often followed by a terrible "low."

Another factor very heavily involved in adolescent suicides is premature sex. Researchers have found a statistical link there. Since the introduction of the Pill and the idea that anything goes as long as "nobody gets hurt," there has been a 300 percent rise in the teenage suicide rate.

I'm embarrassed to admit this, but I'm thinking of committing suicide. I think all the time about how sorry my girlfriend would be for dropping me, and how all my friends would be sad, and my parents would realize they should have been nicer to me. No one would ever forget me.

It shows how little you loved your girlfriend that you would hope to saddle her for life with a guilt trip. And you'd like to make your parents feel guilty for the rest of their days. You must be very angry at all of them.

Actually, these are rather juvenile notions of immortality and power. For example, your girlfriend may feel sorry for you for a while, but then you'll be buried and forgotten with everybody else in the cemetery. She'll go on to live a rewarding life with somebody else and put you in the past, fast.

Life does go on.

Like you, people have two good reasons for killing themselves. (As I've said, nobody does bad things except for good reasons.)

One, they're going to teach everybody a lesson. The pedagogical impulse is very strong in suicidal persons; they want to teach people a lesson. Unfortunately, this is an ineffective way to teach. Yes, survivors are sorry—it's a shame that you have to be buried. Their sorrow lasts, but then people have to get on with their lives, too. There are jobs to be done, bills to be paid.

Two, suicidal people want to end their pain. True, ending pain is a noble profession; anesthesiologists and other medical doctors are rightly honored for ending pain. But suicide doesn't just end pain, it ends life.

In your case, though, you seem to want to inflict pain. So I urge you to go see a counselor about your anger toward your girlfriend, parents, and other people you fantasize about punishing with your death. It's urgent you consult a mental health professional right away. Tell him or her exactly what you've said in this note, and bounce these ideas around a bit.

A counselor will help you deal creatively with the pain you are feeling—and the anger. This can be one of the great moments of growth in your life. A lot of people have felt as you do at some point in their lives—and would today tell you how happy they are they did not act on those feelings.

Get help immediately.

The theme song of one of my favorite TV shows goes, "Suicide Is Painless . . ." Is that true?

That depends on your method. Certain poisons are not painless. Some people put a bullet in themselves and don't die immediately; that's not painless.

Suicide certainly is not painless for the people around you. We're all diminished by the loss of any one of us. Your family will be pained and will be left a legacy of wondering why you did so senseless and stupid a thing. Your friends will wonder why you didn't share your feelings with them.

They will be deeply hurt. There's always pain in the community at the loss of one of its members. I'm not acquainted with the song you mention, but I have no hesitation in telling you the song is wrong.

9

Sexuality

9

What's the purpose of sex?

I've often thought the creation of sex is a testimony to God's sense of humor. But in animal terms sex has the basic purpose of propagating the species.

Human beings carry it further: the genital expression of sexuality is one way we express our commitment to one another and one of the ways we nurture one another.

So, for us, there are two purposes of sex: it unites us in a bond of love and commitment, and it provides us children.

What is the pleasure of sex?

A lot of people don't get pleasure from sex. That may come as a surprise to you, but there are many marriages without sexual activity. And outside of marriage, many kids who have experimented with it say, "It ain't much."

It's a mistake to think all sex is pleasurable, because a lot of it isn't. I'm not even talking about rape, which is an act of brutal aggression and violence, not sex. I'm talking about the many people (including teenagers) who have sex in situations that don't have much to do with love, good feelings, or pleasure.

Pleasurable sensations depend upon the people involved. We're really talking about the total human being. People are sexed from the hair on their heads to the tips of their toes. Every cell in your body is sexed. The amount of pleasurable response—of energy given and received in the sexual act—

depends totally on your feelings of well-being about yourself, your understanding of what it means to be a man or a woman in the world, your understanding of the masculine or feminine in yourself, and your willingness to be open and loving and intimate in this act. The more open, trusting, loving, and intimate you are, the more pleasurable your response will be. Sexual pleasure—because it truly signifies total giving of self—is at its highest inside the context of a permanent commitment.

What is an orgasm? How does it feel for men? Is it different for women?

You're putting the cart before the horse. Orgasmic response is as variable for men as for women. There are nonorgasmic males and nonorgasmic females.

For a woman, orgasm is a heightened sense of pleasure when she reaches a peak of excitement and release. For a man, orgasm is closely identified with ejaculation, but is not the same. Some men ejaculate but don't have orgasms. Others—such as paraplegics—cannot have erections or ejaculations, but may have orgasms.

And some men have very low-level orgasms, some women have big ones. Or vice versa. The more open and loving and intimate you are, the more safe you feel in your relationship, the more orgasmic your response will be.

Westerners know very little about orgasm because they tend to technologize it. Especially in this goal-oriented society, people learn to get the act over with as fast as possible. They think of orgasm as the end point they're striving for, but orgasmic responses, when handled properly, can go on for hours. Most Americans don't know that. In adolescence they learn to mishandle sex entirely. To think of sexual pleasure only in terms of the genitals is a major error. The whole person is involved.

Does sex hurt?

A very unhappy seventeen-year-old girl came to see me one day. I looked at her and wondered what could be wrong. She was young and beautiful, with blond hair and lovely blue eyes. She was athletic, and her personality was delightful.

But in one painful five-minute episode in the backseat of a car, she had lost her virginity, contracted the incurable ailment called herpes simplex II, and had become pregnant. Sex had been very painful for her, indeed.

Physically, the first few acts of sexual intercourse are painful for many women. For others, not so painful. Much depends upon how tense and fearful one is. A woman normally will not be tense and fearful in a situation and with a man she totally trusts. Such trust usually comes only in the deep commitment of marriage.

A teenager's hurried, furtive, guilty sexual acts, in contrast, are not only often painful physically for the girl for whom it is an early experience, but painful, too, in their emptiness. A girl usually ends up saying "It ain't much" after her boyfriend ejaculates prematurely or thrusts a few times and finishes. The girl asks, "Is that all there is to it?" And the boy goes to his buddies boasting how he "scored."

Even when physically good, sexual intercourse between young, unmarried people is emotionally painful. They cannot remain together to share their delight in their physical union; they must break up and return to their different homes.

And then they have to fear pregnancy. A million girls last year got pregnant without a married partner. The pain grew worse when they were forced to make a choice among terrible options: abortion, giving up the child for adoption, keeping the child and probably dropping out of school, or making a hasty, teenage marriage—the kind with an 85 percent divorce rate within two years.

Hundreds of thousands of girls last year faced the later pain of coming down with a sexually transmitted disease. STDs, if left untreated, can have serious consequences. Unfortunately, many show only mild symptoms (or none at all) in women.

So, sex *can* hurt people in a lot of different ways—but it is potentially one of the most enjoyable, pleasurable events in life, when two people who have totally committed themselves to one another in their maturity are expressing that lifelong love.

How should we release sexual feelings, if not through sex?

Sexual feelings are just feelings. They do not demand genital expression. No male need worry his erection will back up and kill him. It will not turn blue and fall off. Nor will it explode. Left alone, it will just limp away.

Often a boy will have nocturnal emissions, accompanied by wildly erotic dreams (better than any masturbatory fantasy) and ejaculate in his sleep. For girls, whose sexuality is more generalized, there is no equivalent.

Why is it wrong for everybody under eighteen to have sex?

Adolescence is when you're putting yourself together, finding out who you are, who God is, what the universe is about, what you want to do with your life, how you relate to other people, what your talents are, and so on.

Sex, if it has meaning, occurs in a loving relationship in which you give yourself away intimately to another human being. That's what the act is about.

If you give yourself away when you're seventeen years

old, you shut down all those questions you're supposed to be asking. You are saying, "I may not know who I am, but I'm giving myself away anyway. Here, I'm yours and you're mine."

That's why it is that 85 percent of the divorces in this country are between couples who married when one or both of them were teenagers. Half of the marriages that shatter each year involve people under 24 at the time of the divorce.

And those are only the marriages. What about all the engagements, the couples "going steady," the intense relationships crumbling upon the insecure foundation of sexual involvement?

These are people who made premature—immature—decisions to give themselves away, when they weren't put together in the first place. If you don't know who you are, how can you love, and therefore know, someone else?

If you don't find out who you are now, you may wait twenty years until the children are raised and then say, "Well, I've finally got to find out who I am. I'm going through a mid-life crisis, and I want to be my own person." I've seen forty-five-year-old executives quit high-paying jobs, leave their wives and children, and move across the country, saying, "I've got to find myself!" That was the basic task they were supposed to have finished between the ages of sixteen and twenty-one.

Giving yourself away early leaves you without the answers to your major questions—and that's a severe liability to carry around. These unanswered questions can end up ruining your future life.

And, of course, babies and other lifelong consequences can result from premature sex; it's dangerous to play with sex outside marriage.

Most girls who become pregnant don't stay in school—

they should—but instead enter the ranks of the unemployed or the underpaid for the rest of their days. We have less information about teenage fathers because most of them leave the consequences of their actions to be dealt with by the girl and her family. That's why I think teenagers playing with sex are like infants handling nitroglycerin.

My parents say it is impossible for adolescents to be truly in love. Is that true?

Whole libraries are devoted to love, so it's not a subject with a snap answer. I wrote a novel about Dante Alighieri; at the age of eight he fell in love with Beatrice. His love informed and inspired his whole life, although they never married one another and she died when he was 24. So the question of age and love is difficult to answer.

But adolescents very often mistake infantile things for love. You might look at someone and think, "Oh, when I'm around her I feel smart and witty and strong" or "I don't have to be smart and witty and strong, because I can depend on him to do those things." So you say, "Gee, I'm in love! And she (or he) seems to like me, too!"

That's not love. That's neurotic dependency. It's built on the notion that someone else will bring these things to you.

You may think, "Oh, he's perfect! Everything he does is perfect! My heart palpitates when I'm near him!" You lose your appetite and can think only of your all-virtuous beloved.

That's not love, either. These are symptoms of "projection," a fantasy projected on someone else.

In what psychologists call "projective love" you don't see someone as they really are. You put up a kind of movie screen in front of him or her and project on that screen a notion of perfection.

Thus, if you're projecting your own feelings, and at the same time imagining all the things your beloved is bringing to you and all the ways he or she makes you feel good, then you are missing the truth about that person twice over. Your love is really self-love projected outward.

That's what usually constitutes "romantic love." So it's no surprise so many marriages based on romantic love fail. It was this state that George Bernard Shaw was describing in the passage I quoted earlier.

Real love is something different from being "in love" in that way. When you really love someone, you know him or her thoroughly—faults *and* virtues. You're an ordinary human being, and the one you love is an ordinary human being. You are best friends. You share some interests, but don't share others. You eat well and your heart doesn't palpitate, but at the same time you will each other's good with a commitment stronger than death. You commit yourself to his or her welfare. You're going to go through the future together facing adventures good, bad, and indifferent —but you'll have them together. You'll have adventures neither of you could know alone. A love relationship is a relationship of mutual growth. Each is helping the other to develop his or her talents, to be all that he or she can be. The welfare and happiness of the other is a primary concern.

Will you ever forget a first love?

It depends on how well your memory functions and whether or not you want to forget. Some first "loves" are such nightmares we're happy to repress any memory of them.

How can you find out if a boy is really in love with you, even if he seems totally honest when he says he is?

You're not a mind reader. But when you say no, does he respect it? Or does he argue, "Why not?" That's your clue.

Does he encourage you to be all you can? To do your best in school, in extracurricular sports and activities? Does he cooperate with his parents and yours in setting boundaries? In other words, how much he really looks out for your welfare is how much he cares about you.

Watch out if he tends to grasp at you and say, "Well, I love you, and therefore you should do this for me" and "I love you, therefore you should do that for me."

If he says, "If you love me, you would," then he's not interested in you, he's interested in himself. Cut him off, dump him fast, cut your losses.

What do you do if there's more love on one side than on the other?

I'm a psychotherapist, and I deal in love a lot. I deal in hate, anger, guilt, depression, and pain. But mostly I deal in love or lack of love.

But I don't know how you can measure someone's love, except by his or her behavior. You know people don't love you if they slug you. You know people don't love you if they only want their way in everything. Love doesn't think in terms of getting, but of giving.

So it is very difficult to decide whether there is more love on one side or another; it's all basically how you behave with each other. If one of you is treating the other badly, that other has a right to demand different treatment—or to break off the relationship

Can jealousy be a healthy emotion?

In "machismo" cultures, jealousy is sometimes seen as a sign of love. How jealous I get shows how much I love you.

But jealousy basically is possessive: I own you; I fear I'm going to lose you. By definition, jealousy implies insecurity and is never really healthy.

That's true of lovers, and it's even true of fathers. Some fathers are jealous of new babies because their wives have less time for them; a baby demands a lot of attention. But jealousy of a baby is a sign of a man's insecurity as a male, a husband, and a human being. Jealousy, in all cases, is a sign of low self-esteem.

If you don't expect us to drink, do drugs, or have sex, what should we do?

You could do your homework.

In a time of life when American young people have the immense privilege—a privilege most people on earth can't dream of enjoying—of reading history, philosophy, fiction, biography, they say, "There's nothing to do."

At a time of life—before they enter business or profession and have little time for anything else—when they can devote their attention to learning about the world of ideas, human beings, great men and women, the past, the arts, in short, the things that make life civilized and worth living, they say, "There's nothing to do."

At a time when young people are subsidized—often totally subsidized—to do nothing but learn, and they have free access to campus libraries with thousands of books on any conceivable topic (including those forbidden in many other nations), they say, "There's nothing to do."

They can extend their life experience, enjoy lives other

than their own, participate in whole epics by reading *War and Peace, Crime and Punishment, Hamlet,* or *The Odyssey.* Fantastic things occur as you live other lives during your luxurious period of schooling.

After you graduate, you will find yourself much too preoccupied with chores, with meeting the mortgage and health insurance payments, and so on, to devote such concentrated time to the history of ideas, the story of our culture, and the whole of human learning.

After this, if you want to enjoy the adventures of the spirit, you'll have to settle for dribs and drabs—a week or two for a book on coffee breaks, or just before bed, or sitting in the barbershop.

It's an impoverished person who has to rely upon drugs, booze, or sex in order to fill time, because life is not drugs, booze, or sex.

A forty-five-year-old woman was having trouble with her daughter. She had grown up in a poor district in Ireland and had not had your opportunities, so one day I said, "I want you to take yourself and your daughter to the ballet." I gave her two tickets for the War Memorial Opera House in San Francisco.

They went. They were stunned by the beauty of the building—the coffered ceilings, the huge pillars, the tremendous light standards and chandeliers.

And then the ballet! It was the most exquisite thing they had ever seen. It was like visiting a new land together. Now they had something wonderful they had shared and could talk about.

Anytime you don't have anything to do, pick up a book. Try writing a book of your own. Start oil painting. Actually listen to a symphony. Or go to the ballet. Join a youth group at your church. Get involved in the school play, go out for some sport. Try enjoying your friends without artificial stimulation.

Why are parents so concerned about what goes on in your social life?

Because your social life can kill you. If your social life includes drinking or drugs, it can physically kill you; if it includes sex, it can give you diseases or make you pregnant and thereby kill your future. If it includes friends who are bad for you, it can kill you both ways.

I've discussed drugs and sex already. Why do I add your friends to this list? Because, as the old saying goes, "He who lies down with dogs gets up with fleas." Your friends can lift you up or tear you down, help you build yourself as a better human being or drag you down to their level.

Not long ago, near Boston, a very bright, well-liked, and academically active teenage girl made a new girlfriend at school. The second girl was severely depressed and into heavy rock music. She had been seeing a therapist.

Apparently, in this case good did not triumph over evil, a good mood did not win over a bad mood, a happy person could not resist the drag of a depressed person.

In a few weeks, the two girls committed suicide in the same bedroom, leaving a note filled with rock music lyrics.

Your parents were once teenagers. They know your friendships can lead you astray.

I feel that having a boyfriend doesn't mean I'm bad or anything. It's a part of growing up. But my mom feels differently. Is there anything wrong with having a boyfriend or girlfriend?

If by "boyfriend" you mean you have a friend of the opposite sex, wonderful.

But if you mean you're having sex, no wonder your mother is distressed.

I would advise you to have lots of friends of both sexes at this time of your life. It is part of growing up. Don't miss out by tying your social life to only one person.

How late should teenagers be allowed to stay out?

It depends on the maturity of the individual. Maturity varies from person to person. So curfew time is negotiated between parents and their children.

When I visit high schools, young people always ask how to negotiate curfew. This is what I say:

First, when does the discussion on curfew normally take place? When Sally is about to go out the door, with Lunkhead leaning on the horn of his pickup parked in the driveway?

On the way out, Sally walks by Dad sitting in the front room and says, "Dad, is it all right if I stay out an hour later tonight?"

Dad looks out at Lunkhead, still leaning on his horn, and immediately thinks, *sex!* He sees Lunkhead sitting, not in a pickup truck, but in a portable shelter for the seduction of other people's daughters. *"No!"* he yells in panic.

Sally catches the threat in his voice. "Why not?"

"Because I said so!" Dad doesn't want to say precisely why not—it might give her ideas.

"Well, what the heck, just an extra hour . . . I have every right . . . and everybody's . . . all my friends get to . . ." Sally argues.

Dad jumps up and yells, "No! I said, No! You come back on time, or else you'll be grounded for a month!"

Sally charges out with her belly churning. Dad sits down again with his tummy turning, thinking, "I hope she comes back on time; I don't want to have to punish her."

Three things in that story should be corrected:

First, as I said earlier, if you're going to communicate, you have to sit down. You can't communicate while running, going in a different directions, standing up, walking around, or leaving.

Second, Sally is talking about time; Dad, about sex. In order to communicate you have to try to talk about the same thing.

Third, any girl whose date leans on the horn rather than ringing the doorbell and greeting the parents should dump him right away, because he is a grade-A loser.

How can Sally turn this around?

She should remember her father is being the best parent he can. Anybody with kids wants to be a good parent. He wants his kids to love him, and he tries to love his kids. Some parents don't do a very good job of it, but I never met a parent who wasn't doing the best he or she knew how.

So, in trying to raise her parents with greater understanding, Sally needs to catch Dad right after he has just resolved to be the best parent in the world. That, normally, is on the way home from church services.

At that time, Sally says, "Dad, it's been eight months since the curfew was set at so-and-so time. I'm eight months older. I've been very responsible. I haven't broken the curfew once. Since I've been really good about it, I'd like to move it to such-and-such time."

Dad, of course, promptly asks, "Where are you going?"

"I'm not going anywhere. I'm talking about time."

"Why are we talking about it now?" Dad asks.

"Because this is the best time to talk about it, when I'm not charging out the door or something; I want to talk about time," Sally answers. She's kept it on the right topic: time. Not sex, not Lunkhead, not the car horn.

"Well, I don't know," Dad says reluctantly. He has something on his mind other than time.

Now Sally says, "Well, tell me what you're afraid I might do in that extra hour that I couldn't do beforehand."

Dad hems and haws. He won't tell her.

"Well, tell me what it is that you used to do in that extra hour, and I'll promise not to do that, because you must be thinking of something I might do."

Dad won't tell her that either. Sally's got him in a corner.

"Well, what about it? For eight months I've proven very responsible, and I think as sort of a reward we should add an extra hour to my curfew time," Sally says.

Dad will probably agree. There's no where else to go. He's just decided to be a good parent; Sally's shown herself a responsible youngster; they've been talking about the proper issue, time; and Sally has been honest and straightforward. Sally will probably get her extra hour.

Trying to negotiate curfew at the last moment before going out is usually going to end in failure.

How do you deal with parents who want to know about your sexual involvement?

I don't recall having walked up to my children and asked, "Are you still a virgin?" There are oversuspicious parents who project their own fantasies upon what their young people are doing. They don't respect their children's privacy and dignity. Everyone has a right to answer, "I don't want to go into that."

On the other hand, your parents may be concerned for your welfare. If my teenaged daughter were unmarried, pregnant, and living at home I'd surely have some questions, because we need to understand the ramifications. Or if she came down with venereal disease, I'd surely want to know whether she got infected from promiscuous behavior, or from one certain person, and whether she had reported him. Some discussion would be in order.

Your parents should respect your privacy, but at a certain point you need their guidance, support, and protection more than you need privacy. It's a difficult balance you and your parents have to try to work out yourselves. If they simply want to discuss your attitudes, meet them halfway.

How can I bring up the subject of sex with my parents without getting embarrassed or being lectured? This is what they always say: "You better not come home pregnant."

They're also implying you can do anything short of getting pregnant. Try casually remarking to your mother, "Mom, do you realize how often I'm told I better not come home pregnant?—as if I can do anything I want to do as long as I don't get pregnant?"

Use some of the pointers on communications mentioned earlier, and, instead of talking directly about sex, ask your mother about her social life and experiences with boys before she met your father. That may lead naturally into the question you want to ask her.

How can we, the new generation, live our life with our own sexual views without hurting our parents?

You probably won't have to hurt your parents. If your sexual views are healthy and take into account the whole of your personhood, they will tend to be like your parents'.

Traditional sexual values are traditional because they've been proven through the ages. True, we went through a period of insanity in the late 1960s and early 1970s when apostles of sexual freedom ran about preaching the glories of promiscuity. We even had a book called *Open Marriage* claiming that if you were broad-minded and sophisticated enough, you could have extramarital affairs. But today the same people are returning to moderate, and monogamous lifestyles. Indeed, one of the former proponents of "open marriage" now preaches deepened, committed monogamous relationships.

Those values that tend to survive the test of time are based on a true understanding of human nature. Sexual fidelity seems an example. It builds the most positive foundation for complete fulfillment for both partners. (Polygamous cultures tend, in contrast, to emphasize the fulfillment of one partner over others.)

I think of the teenage girl I mentioned earlier—the one who lost her virginity, got herpes, and became pregnant all on the same evening. Her anguished face as she described her worries about the baby she's carrying contrasts so sharply with that of the young wife of twenty as she radiates delight in the circle of her rejoicing friends during a baby shower that I cannot doubt traditional values have something to offer.

My mom told me that sex isn't very much fun, but it's something husbands have to have. She said sex can be very lonely for women. Is that true?

It's true that your mother isn't having much fun sexually. It would appear your father demands it as a biological necessity. Obviously, for them, it isn't lovemaking.

I said earlier that there are many marriages lacking pleasurable sexual activity. But there are many for whom genital intercourse is the most pleasurable way they communicate their love, a beautiful, even mystical experience of total loving. Instead of feeling "lonely," such couples experience true communion.

Lately in therapy it's been the women who are hungry for more sexual loveplay. Their husbands seem more interested in television, work, or football. As one aggressive salesman told me, "I only do it to please her; I don't get anything out of it." Indeed, in a recent survey of 1,550 men and women eighteen and older, 68 percent said watching television gave them "a great deal of pleasure and satisfaction," as contrasted with sexual relationships which got only a 42 percent score.

In fact, they said friends (61%), helping others (59%), vacations (58%), hobbies (56%), and reading (55%) were more emotionally important to them than sex.

However, it sounds as though your mother and father should seek therapeutic help. The sexual aspect of their married life is in disrepair. Therapy might help your mother discover many joys she's been missing.

Because she felt free enough to tell you that, you should feel free to show her this response.

How do I keep my parents from knowing I am sexually active?

I find it interesting that your activity is such that you feel you have to keep it secret.

Consider a married couple. We all assume they're having sex. They're not ashamed of it. They don't feel they have to keep it secret.

You should question a relationship that has to be kept a secret. It's a good rule not to do things of which you're not going to be proud.

What do I do when my parents don't trust me when I am with a friend of the opposite sex?

If you look at your parents' distrust as a sign of their fear for your welfare, you can better appreciate what they're trying to say. Try to reassure them. One young girl in my office turned to her mother and said, "Mom, you raised me right, I'm not going to do anything that would harm me, my future or my family." Perhaps you could try something like that approach.

What do I do when my girl's parents don't let me see her?

Well, if you truly love her, don't do anything to get her in trouble with her parents. It's not good for her to be estranged from her parents.

Cool it. Time is on your side. One day soon she'll be eighteen and free to see you. If your love can't stand the test of time, it's not love.

If you encourage her to defy her parents, you are not thinking of her, but yourself. Doing that means you don't love her.

My parents and I constantly argue about how often my boyfriend and I should see each other. He is nineteen, and even so, nothing will happen sexually. They don't seem to understand this. How can I get them to understand, and extend my curfew?

It depends on how old you are. If you're sixteen, your parents are quite right to be concerned. Nineteen-year-old boys tend to have ideas a sixteen- or seventeen-year-old girl isn't ready for.

But if you're nineteen, you probably shouldn't have a curfew at all, because you're at an age when you can set your own sensible limits.

Look at your parents' motivation. If they are trying to protect you from harm and nurture your growth, they're probably being very sensible.

If they think your relationship with your boyfriend is hurting your grades or the extracurricular activities that make you a well-rounded person, then they're probably right.

If they disapprove of his character, let yourself dwell on their doubts. See if there's any truth to them. Don't blindly dismiss them on the grounds he's perfect.

What about seeing if he can come on family outings with you? That way, you could see each other and your parents would be assured nothing sexual is happening.

How should you react when your parents walk in on you and your date?

With delight, since your parents are friends of yours, I would hope. Presumably they will have walked in on you having friendly conversation, a cup of coffee, or a bowl of popcorn or watching TV.

If you have been engaged in sexual activity of which you're ashamed, your own reaction is telling you something.

How far is it all right for you to go if you're able to control yourself and not go all the way?

"Controlling yourself" is one of the great fallacies of all time.

One of the things that often happens between a boy and a girl in adolescence is they begin to escalate their relationship. It begins with kissing and petting above the waist, and then pretty soon that's not satisfying enough. The petting moves below the waist, but then that's not satisfying enough either. Soon they ask, "Well, if we can go this far, why not further?" And passion takes over.

Very few people are so cold-blooded that in the middle of high sexual passion they can stop easily. That's why a million young girls become pregnant each year.

Most such girls thought they could control themselves. That's one of the reasons they didn't prepare themselves for sexual intercourse. Neither did the seventeen-year-old girl I mentioned earlier. She didn't come prepared for sex, and neither did her date. They got "carried away."

A million girls a year is a huge number. It's a huge number of babies. Many are aborted, more are put up for adoption or kept. That means we have a huge number of children raising children. Almost every one of those mothers thought they could control themselves and not "go all the way." They found out they were wrong.

What are some romantic ways to get closer to your boyfriend without having sex?

Romance and intimacy is one thing; sex and sexual intimacy, another. You want to get to know one another on the levels of friendship, intellect, spirit, and emotion. The best way to do that is to share experiences. Double-date with another responsible couple; go to parties and sports events with groups of people. That way you'll forestall sexual adventures and keep your friendship growing.

Very often when a relationship becomes sexual—even among adults having affairs—people begin getting together only for sex. The other areas in their relationship stop developing and soon begin to decay.

I counseled a very tragic case like this.

The girl was very bright. In her freshman year in high school she was a class officer. She was an all-around athlete, and she earned straight A's. She hoped to run for student body president later in her high school career.

In her sophomore year of high school she attracted the notice of a senior boy (Sophomore year is a dangerous, romantic year for girls; they seem particularly susceptible to older boys then.) She was very flattered by the attentions of this upperclassman. Soon they were dating steadily, often excluding anybody else. They became sexually active.

The boy persuaded her not to run for student office in her sophomore year because it would take too much time away from their relationship. Then he used the same reason to talk her into resigning one of her team sports. Her grades dropped to a B average. Her parents, seeing what was happening, tried to help. Their disapproval of the boy only made her cling more tightly to him.

By her junior year, the long conversations, the shared experiences, the levity and friendship, had stopped. Her boyfriend would take her to a movie and afterward, in the car, have intercourse with her. He would take her out somewhere else—and have intercourse. That was now the only reason for getting together.

Her boyfriend talked her into dropping her two remaining sports activities, because they, too, took time away from "them." By the end of her junior year, she had no other boyfriends and was involved in no student activities or sports; her grades had dropped drastically.

It got worse her senior year. He had graduated from high school and had found a part-time job. He met her each day after school. She was his sex object and playmate, and she had no other friends. She was depressed by the relationship, but she didn't know how to get out of it, because she was so sexually involved with him.

Finally, over the protests of her boyfriend, she managed to be accepted by a college away from her home city. "Moving to another city was my way out," she told me. "But it was not any Ivy League school. I was on probation because of my poor high school grades."

Four months later her college roommate called school officials. After days of not eating, drinking, or going to class, she had slashed her wrists. Her parents were notified. They went to her, flew home with her, and brought her to me.

What had triggered her breakdown? A friend had written her that her former boyfriend was dating a junior in her old high school. That letter reminded her of what a jerk he was, and of what she had given up, all she had lost of her youthful friends, dreams, goals, and ideals, in order to meet his sexual demands. The great empty space of her high school years opened before her. She fell in. She fell into a deep depression.

Her adolescence had been meant for her to grow in creative, healthy ways. But by involving herself sexually she had stopped her growth. That realization devastated her.

It took a couple of months of intensive therapy to get her out of her depression, and finally, when she was well enough, she got a job. After some time, she reentered the college to try to start over.

Hearing about experiences like these have convinced me and a number of other sex educators that if you are under eighteen, you are simply not prepared for sexual activity. You aren't put together yet.

Sexual activity is particularly unwise for girls, who bear the brunt of disease and pregnancy, and thus tend to be devastated psychologically by premature sexual involvement. Researchers have found a statistical link between teen suicides and premature sex. When girls and boys give themselves away sexually and the affair breaks up, many are left with profoundly damaged feelings of self-worth.

Sexual activity is not a goal. Sexual activity is not a sign of maturity. Sex is meant to be the expression of a love relationship, and it is at its best only in the context of a committed, lifelong love relationship.

You are very wise to search out ways to be with your boyfriend without getting sexually involved.

Why do girls so often feel they have to give in and satisfy their boyfriends?

If a boy is pressuring you for a yes, you know he doesn't love you.

The ability to say no is one of the things we learn in adolescence. If you cannot say no, your yes isn't worth much. When you say no to someone, that person gets to know you better, learns your boundaries, what you stand for.

If he (or she) tries to invade your boundaries and overcome your no, he doesn't respect you very much. He's only interested in his wants and pleasures, his way in everything. That's not love.

Love means someone wants good things for you—but you're the judge. Someone who loves you, wills your will, wants you to fulfill *your* ambitions and dreams. In the case I mentioned earlier, if that young man truly had loved that girl, he would have encouraged her to be student body president, junior class president, track star, an A student. He would have said, "Your grades are slipping; we'd better see each other less. Your grades are very important, because you want to go to so-and-so college, and I really want you to fulfill your dreams."

And as you learn to say no to others in adolescence, you learn to say no to yourself, too. That's the foundation of self-discipline and self-respect. Nobody gets to tread on you —not even you. No one gets to abuse you—not even you. When you say no, you make it stick. When you say yes, you mean yes.

Many people don't know how to say no, so they say yes but act out no. They say yes and then punish you subtly as they fulfill their promise—so you won't ask them again. That leaves everyone miserable.

Learning no is a great treasure. It makes you a person, not part of a herd. Nobody gets to manipulate you.

Girls who "give in" to "satisfy their boyfriends" are saying they have such low self-esteem that they feel they have to use their bodies to buy companionship. All of this applies equally to boys who are feeling all sorts of pressures to "have sex."

At what age is a person ready to have sex?

In a preceding answer, I said age eighteen, but I really mean you're not ready until you have finished adolescence. Few people finish before eighteen. Many don't finish until twenty-five; they're still dependent on their parents for their tuition and board, or they're living at home or dependent upon their parents in other ways. Until they're able to stand on their own two feet, they are adolescents.

If they're not independent of their families, how can they really know who they are themselves? And if they don't really know who they are, how can they be ready to commit themselves sexually to another person?

Maturity means the ability to handle consequences yourself, without requiring your parents to prop you up. So, when you ask if you are ready for sex, what you should really ask is whether you are ready to father or mother a child. If not, you're not ready for sex.

Never undertake something if you aren't ready to handle the consequences. Don't buy a car if you can't afford the payments. Don't give your promise if you don't want to follow through. And don't have sex with somebody you wouldn't want to be the father or mother of your child. If you do, you're not doing the right thing for yourself or for the other.

If I want to have a sexual relationship, should I go to my parents and ask for birth control, or should I go to an ob-gyn clinic alone?

Ignoring the question of whether a sexual relationship would really be good for you, the answer depends upon how open and how deep your relationship is with your parents.

But you should know that there is no such thing as a perfectly reliable contraceptive; The Pill has side effects so adverse that nearly half the women who try it stop rapidly. The condom has a ten percent failure rate.

I wish high schools would teach all young women the Billing's ovulation method of family regulation. It is not the rhythm method, which has been discredited. It is a method requiring body awareness, by which a young woman knows the exact time of her ovulation.

The ovulation method requires abstinence for six to eight days a month. Some people say, "Oh, abstinence, oh my golly!" But I know of no married couples who, for reasons of work or travel, don't have to abstain periodically anyway. In fact, there is far more abstinence in most marriages than there is sexual abandon.

Anyway, the ovulation method of natural family planning is the only safe, nonsexist, person-enhancing method of birth control, and I recommend it.

If two teenagers are truly in love why shouldn't they have premarital sex?

For teenagers, there is rarely such a thing as "premarital" sex. Teenage sexual intercourse is seldom premarital, that is, "leading to marriage." Teenagers engaging in genital expressions of love are engaging in premature sexual activity. If you are truly in love, you will want to do what is best for your beloved. How will sexual activity—secret, furtive, guilt- and fear-ridden—enhance his or her sense of well-being? Also, are you both ready for fathering and mothering the child that might ensue? If not, why engage in baby-making activities? *No* is a love word.

I'm pregnant. I just told my mom and she's furious. How should I handle this with my parents?

After your mother's fury dies down, she will be sad. And then she will start helping you handle the problem.

Your mother will go through emotions just as if someone in your family had died. First there was denial, perhaps, although it's hard to deny you're pregnant—nobody's a little bit pregnant. Then there was a phase of anger: "Why did this happen? This is awful, dreadful!" (Your mother appears to be in this stage now.) And then there will be sadness and, finally, acceptance.

You see, there has been a kind of loss in your family. A loss of your innocence, for one, but a loss, too, of the girl your mother assumed was free of major problems. The daughter your mother knew is gone. You're going to grow up awfully fast now. When she accepts that, she will be your ally in confronting the major decisions you will have to make.

But imagine how differently your mother would have reacted had you been twenty-three and married a year, announcing your first pregnancy. A celebration would have been planned.

In my practice I confront this problem almost daily, which is why I so firmly urge teenagers not to tamper with their sexual powers until they're prepared to bear the consequences.

If you're pregnant and don't know whether to keep the baby, give it up for adoption, or have an abortion, how should you go about making the decision?

Discuss it with your parents, your clergyman, and an independent adult whose wisdom you trust very much.

Yours is not a decision to be made lightly. No one can make it for you, because you are the one who has to live with the life-long consequences.

I think, however, abortion is the worst choice you can possibly make. Many people argue the religious and moral questions of abortion, but few mention its affect on a woman's psyche; that's left to therapists like me.

I have counseled women who had abortions years ago and were still full of guilt, dismay, and depression. Two of them with the most severe consequences had no moral or religious qualms at the time of the abortion but felt their self-esteem drastically reduced. One woman suffered anxiety attacks every time her current husband brought up the idea of having a baby. She felt she would be an unfit mother, she said, "because I murdered my first baby." It required very extensive work to help her through that.

What about adoption? I've also worked with women who have given up their children for adoption. Intellectually they believed they had done the right thing, but on every birthday of those children they felt deep pangs of loss. I've met women who were fantasizing about the children they had given up long ago.

Keeping the child? This option, too, has long-term consequences. Most girls drop out of school when they have a baby, but then they add undereducation to the problem they already have. There are programs to help you finish high school and maybe even go on to college while bringing

up your child. I have known a few young women to continue their education; their family supported them and accepted the child wholeheartedly as a grandchild or niece or
nephew. And then they later entered successful marriages
with men who were also able to accept the child.

Marrying the father? That's probably not a good option.
Those marriages seldom last, and the father may feel co-
erced. Don't marry the father unless you were already intending marriage before the pregnancy.

My personal view is you should also consider the welfare
of the child growing within you and the impact on both of
you of any of these decisions.

It is not an easy decision; its consequences will be felt by
you for the rest of your life—and your child's life.

*I'm a teenage girl and I hear that it's so terrible to get pregnant and have
a baby, but whenever I see a little baby it's so cute and happy, and it's
a special, warm relationship. What's wrong with having a baby?*

Ask any young mother. Babies do not stay warm, cuddly
little dolls. Their diapers must be changed regularly. They
squall in the middle of the night with colic, or because
they're hungry or wet. They are a 24-hour-a-day, 365-day-
a-year responsibility from which you have no relief. You
cannot do anything—anything—without first taking into
account how the baby will be cared for, what you will do
with it, and whether you will take it with you.

Soon the baby begins to walk and get into things and,
around the age of two, say no to you with great determina-
tion and fight you in the supermarket for candy at the
checkout lane.

Babies don't stay infants in arms. They require enormous
quantities of loving care and attention. And many girls your
age begin to grow angry at their babies for what they've had

to sacrifice for their child. Then, of course, babies later become teenagers.

What should you do if you're a teenager who got someone pregnant?

Don't fade into the woodwork. You are responsible for engendering a child, and you have as true a relationship to it biologically as does the mother. You should become part of the solution to the problem.

All meaningful actions have consequences. Mature people accept and deal with the consequences. Your mature reaction should be not to leave the mother alone with this problem. I don't mean you should necessarily marry her—teenage marriages, as I've said, rarely succeed, and neither you nor the mother need a divorce to go along with a pregnancy.

Simply work as lovingly as you can for the welfare of that mother and child and their future. Stay involved, if at all possible, in the decision making, in supporting the mother of your child at this time of anguish.

What's wrong with getting married at seventeen if you're truly in love?

Nothing morally wrong. But you face huge emotional, practical, and financial responsibilities you might not be ready for.

Let's take one area, the easiest to figure: finances. Suddenly you are responsible for two human beings. If you both work, figure how much you will be earning. Then look at a couple of apartments, and check the cost of one you like, including lights, garbage, water, and the various damage and cleaning deposits.

Once you have that figured on a monthly basis, head for a department store and pretend to furnish and stock the kitchen, bedroom, living room, bathroom. Chances are you've started with the stereo and the couch. Now add in the vacuum cleaner, dish towels, spare linens, toilet cleanser, cups and saucers, clocks.

Then call a health insurance company and find out how much you'll need to insure both of you for hospital care. (A nice, garden variety bout of appendicitis could cost you the price of a new car if you're uninsured.) And if you plan to have a baby, check out maternity coverage, or there goes another new car. What if the wife has a difficult pregnancy and cannot work?

If you don't have a vehicle yet, find out what a used car will cost you. (At seventeen, you probably won't qualify for a new car loan.)

Figure your clothing expenses, and keep track of food bills for each of you for a couple of weeks.

Can the two of you afford to get married?

What's a good age to get married?

Any adult age is a good age to get married, even if you're ninety. Marriage is a commitment for life, a covenant of intimacy. But before you can give yourself away, you have to be financially, emotionally, and spiritually capable of supporting a separate household.

Marriage does not solve your problems but rather gives two people a way to deal with the problems together.

I'm seventeen and mature for my age. I'm in love with a man who's twenty-one. My parents tell me he's too old for me, but I love him anyway. Why can't my relationship work?

If you're seventeen and he's twenty-one, you should wait at least three years before you marry. Seventeen is a highly romantic age. At seventeen your goals and ideals may be very different from his. At seventeen you may not have a realistic appreciation of all the duties, responsibilities, and sheer hard work involved in maintaining a household.

And you're growing fast. Your mental attitude in the next three years will change and grow as much as it did in the last five.

Researchers have recently compiled some of the reasons so many early marriages fail. Let me give you some:

High school marriages fail because 47 percent of them are in hasty response to pregnancy.

They fail because of the immaturity of one or both partners;

because of the breakdown in career and education plans the financial obligations of marriage cause;

because the parents oppose the marriage, and therefore are unwilling to give financial support;

because if one partner continues schooling he or she outgrows the other intellectually, emotionally, and spiritually;

because teenagers often marry to escape from home, a tyrannical parent, or responsibilities.

At seventeen, you should very carefully and honestly look at your motivations. Do any of the above apply to you?

Marriage is one of the largest adult responsibilities you can undertake. You have to create a meaningful relationship with another human being and then maintain it at all costs and through all ups and downs, supporting each other financially, emotionally, and spiritually for the rest of your lives.

Some girls want to marry early so they can escape going to school any longer, or getting a job. They figure, "Well, my husband will support me, and I'll have that lovely little baby." They are completely unaware of the realities of marriage.

Half the early marriages involve a teenage girl marrying

an older boy. She grows a bit, and at twenty she finds herself feeling very differently about this fellow than she did when she was a starry-eyed seventeen.

There's another reason teenage marriages fail. Girls and boys think differently about sex. Adolescent girls fall in love with a name, a face, and a personality. (They often don't view the name, face, and personality realistically, but that's another matter.) They romanticize these features, and that's when they feel sexy.

Boys tend to have erections. They have erections when they wake up in the morning, when they're walking down the school hallway, when they're looking at the stars, when they're lying on the beach—when, in short, they have nobody in mind. Their erections are omnidirectional—they don't point at specific people; they're just there.

Now, the girl—who feels sexy only when she has a person in mind, and she "loves" him—sees his erection and thinks, "Oh! He loves me!"

This is her fundamental mistake. He doesn't love her! He's just had a physiological accident, a physiological "happening." His erection doesn't have a name on it; it isn't pointed toward her personally—it'll point anywhere. Girls very often make the mistake of thinking, "He has an erection and he's sexually interested in me. I'm only sexually interested in people I'm 'in love' with, so he must love me." She and the boy escalate toward sex and then talk marriage.

What happens then? Eventually the sexual aspect of the relationship loses its novelty as the realities of 23-hour-a-day nonsexual life must be confronted. They have to deal with how they're going to pay the bills, who's going to take out the garbage, who's mopping the kitchen floor, who makes the bed, and so on.

A twenty-one-year-old man came to me planning to divorce his eighteen-year-old wife after only a year and a half of marriage. He was going to divorce her because he couldn't stand her sloppiness, carelessness, and irresponsibility. She was driving him out of his mind.

For fifteen minutes he raved about the messiness of the house and the dishes not being washed.

And then he told me what had happened the other day. In the morning his wife said she was going to come down to his office for lunch. At noon he waited for her. He didn't go out for lunch, and, of course, he hadn't brought a lunch with him. But she didn't show up.

Panicked, he phoned home, but there was no answer. He phoned the hospitals, but she wasn't listed. He called everywhere he could think of, but no one had seen her.

Hungry and worried, he stopped work often that afternoon, calling home, thinking an accident must have happened. Distracted, he did poor work, and his supervisor raised hell with him.

Finally at the end of the day he went home. The house was a mess. She was still missing. Worry was driving him crazy. Then his wife waltzed in. It seems a friend of hers had dropped in from out of town, and they had gone off together to do some shopping. She'd just forgotten about the lunch.

He was ranting as he told me this story. I had him breathe slowly for a while and finally got him calmed down.

I said, "You know, eighteen months ago you married this girl because of very good feelings you must have had toward her. But I've heard nothing but negatives and a desire to dump her.

"Go back to the days before you married her. Tell me the good qualities she had that made you love her."

He thought for a few minutes. Then he said, "Well, she was so spontaneous and carefree."

She was the same girl. The same quality he once thought of as "spontaneous and carefree" he now described as "sloppy, irresponsible, and careless." The difference was now he was married to it.

Here's another example. A woman brought in her husband. After nine years of marriage and three children, she intended to divorce him. Why? Because he didn't communicate, didn't talk, didn't react. There was no emotional intimacy.

"When he goes to a party," she said, "he sits on the sofa and doesn't talk to anyone. He's so shy," she went on, "he's going to lose his job."

I looked at him. He was sitting there, in my office, not saying a word. So I turned to her again and asked her what she had seen in him that caused her to marry him.

She pondered this. "Well," she said, "he was such a good listener, the strong, silent type."

Another: a businesswoman came in intending to divorce her husband of twenty years. She told me all he did was sit around the swimming pool, which, by the way, she had paid for. Throughout their marriage, he had stayed at home, tended the kids, and daydreamed about winning the lottery. All he did was drink beer with his friends around the pool.

She was tired of his sloth. She had tried to involve him in her business, and each time within a week she had fired him because he was more trouble than he was worth.

"What was he doing when you met him?" I asked her.

"Well, he was a surfer at Oahu."

"Oh? Well, even surfers at Oahu have to support themselves. What was he doing for money?" I asked.

"He was living off an inheritance left by his grandmother."

"Ah," I said, "let me get this straight: You married a man

who was living off the money of a woman and lying around the beach drinking beer with his friends. And now you want to divorce him because he is living off the money of a woman (you) and lying around the swimming pool drinking beer with his friends."

"Well," she said, "I thought marriage would change him."

"Marriage," I answered, "never changes anybody except for the worse."

I meant this: if you are thinking of marrying, look at your proposed partner and cut in half the virtues you see. (Everybody who is wooing anybody is on his or her best behavior.) Then double the vices you see. Now you probably have a more realistic picture of what your partner is like.

So, to answer your question, the longer you wait, the more likely you'll see the truth about your older boyfriend.

And in the meantime, don't miss out on opportunities for learning about other boys. It's crucial you get as wide a social experience with other people as you possibly can.

You might want to compromise with your parents and say, "Is it all right if I see him occasionally while I date other people also?"

Is it all right for a teenage boy to have sex with an older woman?

The "older woman" may be prosecuted for child molestation or contributing to the delinquency of a minor, depending upon the situation.

Is masturbation harmful?

Not if you are referring to the old scare stories. Masturbation will not cause you to "go crazy"; it will not cause hair to grow on the palms of your hands; it will not harm your childbearing prospects.

Masturbation can sometimes lead to marital problems, however. Some females who have masturbated a great deal find it difficult to have an orgasm except through direct manual clitoral stimulation. This can be frustrating to them and their husbands.

Because masturbation is usually done in a hidden and hurried fashion, males tend to condition their sexual machinery to rapid action, and thus educate themselves to be premature ejaculators. Or they achieve full delight only when they do it for themselves, not when they're inside the vagina of their wives. These are possible problems for people who have masturbated over a long period of time.

Also, if you masturbate to the degree you are interested mostly in yourself, isolating yourself from other people and making masturbation do for normal social contact, then it can be socially harmful to you.

My parents think I'm anti social (maybe even gay) just because I don't get dates.

The implication you're gay simply because you're not interested in dating yet is horrendous. It's not necessarily so. Different people mature at different rates.

Why are you reluctant to date? Are you shy? There's nothing wrong with being shy. But you might want to risk getting out of your shyness.

If you're afraid of people of the opposite sex, there's only one way of overcoming it: by putting your toe in the water in the shallow end of the pool.

Discuss with your parents what they expect of you and what's worrying them. Don't accept any labels. And remember that you are in an exciting time of life. You can meet many people of the opposite sex on a nonthreatening level. Go at your own comfortable pace on this. Your parents' situation is the envy of many thousands of parents who wish their teenagers would expand their horizons beyond dating.

I'm nineteen, male, and think I'm gay: I'm in love with a friend (who's normal). He doesn't know I feel this way. I have never been even slightly attracted to girls, but I've always loved guys. I haven't told anybody, and I don't know what to do, although this is very painful for me. What should I do?

Don't make sexual advances toward your friend, who is probably heterosexual, because that would probably frighten him away and he would no longer be your friend.

And, instead of living in silent agony, seek counseling so you can learn more about yourself. A therapist will not try to change your orientation but will help you determine whether you truly are homosexual.

Homosexuality is no longer considered a mental disorder by counselors. Instead, your counseler will treat it as a problem you have in finding out what your sexual orientation is and dealing with it in a way that won't be destructive to you.

How do you know if you have VD?

First, the term VD (venereal disease) is being replaced by another, STD (sexually transmitted disease). You don't necessarily know if you have certain STD's—and that's serious because untreated STDs can cause very severe health problems. A chlamydia infection, for example, is often transmitted at the same time as gonorrhea and the gonorrhea "masks" the chlamydia. If you even suspect you might have caught an STD, go to your doctor immediately. He or she will keep your visit confidential. If you don't have a regular physician, look up your local health department's STD clinic. I am not going to give you a course on medicine here, but it might do to know some of the symptoms of the various STDs so if you've been sexually active, you can watch out for them.

Gonorrhea in men used to be easily detectable within five days because the fellow had a yellow/green discharge, suffered pain during urination, and, if he didn't treat it, began to urinate blood. I say "used to be" because now we've got some new, not so detectable, "super" strains of gonorrhea. These "super" strains are also resistant to the penicillin treatments that are used to knock out the more usual gonorrheal infection.

Gonorrhea in women is less easy to detect. About four out of five women who have it don't notice its earliest symptoms because the discharge may be masked by vaginal secretions, menstrual flow, and so forth. Pain during urination may be a warning, as well as pain in the pelvic region. If the infection is untreated in women it has the potential of damaging the Fallopian tubes and rendering the woman sterile. Since most gonorrhea is found in women under twenty-one, that's bad news.

Syphilis shows up in both men and women as sores, lumps, or blisters around the penis, the vulva, or the anus. Syphilis is curable but it is important to get diagnosed and treated as soon as possible, before it has done any further damage to you and before you've passed it on.

You will know you have herpes simplex II when you develop little red patches that burn and itch. Blisters will appear, which then break into painful ulcers. These symptoms show up in the genital areas of both men and women. The usual attack clears up in a week or ten days, but it can be extremely painful. The time between outbreaks varies from person to person. There is as yet no cure for herpes simplex II, but your doctor can give you some helpful treatments. Your doctor must carefully monitor you if you are pregnant, since herpes simplex II can cause premature delivery, miscarriage, or serious damage to the infant should it catch the disease.

The basic symptom of the STD chlamydia trachomatis is pain in the pelvic region. It is responsible for over half the ectopic pregnancies in the United States.* (In an ectopic pregnancy the child grows in the Fallopian tube rather than the womb. It always results in the death of the child, and it kills one out of every one thousand mothers who experience it. The other 999 will probably never produce a living child.) Chlamydia trachomatis causes chronic lifelong pain for 15 to 20 percent of the women who get it.

AIDS is a fatal disease that is most prevalent in the United States among homosexuals and bisexuals. When it shows up in heterosexuals, it is generally among drug addicts employing used needles or among persons who received contaminated blood products. The initial symptoms of AIDS are nonspecific and similar to the symptoms of simple colds, bronchitis, or stomach flu. In AIDS, however, these symptoms continue or keep recurring. The general symptoms include: unexplained, persistent fatigue; unexplained, persistent fever, or drenching night sweats; unexpected weight loss of greater than ten pounds; swollen glands (lymph nodes); unexplained creamy white patches on the tongue or mouth; persistent diarrhea; and unexplained persistent, frequent dry cough.

The best way of finding out if you have an STD is to go to a doctor immediately and say, "I fear that I have an STD

---

*See Louis Weinstein, M.D., "Ectopic Pregnancy: Growing Threat of the 1980s," *Medical Aspects of Human Sexuality* 19, no. 9 (September 1985).

and I would like a checkup for this." Doctors respect confidentiality.

Get a doctor's opinion as soon as the fear strikes you; otherwise you will live with an unresolved fear, which can be crippling. It is much better to have the truth. If your examination shows you don't have a sexually transmitted disease, you will have peace of mind. If you do have an STD, the sooner you start treatment, the better.

10

On Parents, Schoolwork,
and
Other Questions

10

When you're doing poorly in a sport or a subject, and your parents think you're doing really well, what's the best way to tell them?

Sit them down and say, "I have something to tell you. I'm not really doing well at this sport" (or "I'm really having trouble in this course").

They're going to find out sooner or later, and you're better off being the first to tell them. The truth will set you free. If they have to find out for themselves, you run the risk of severely damaging their trust in you.

If you're having trouble in a subject, they might be able to get you tutoring or help you at home. If you're having trouble in a sport, why are you playing it? Perhaps you could choose another.

If you have been telling your parents falsehoods all along, now's the time to be truthful with them. Otherwise it will be quite a jolt when they get your report card or see you benched at the big game. If you tell them now, perhaps they can help you to get a better grade or select another sport.

How can I learn to do better in school?

In school you have a wonderful opportunity to learn about everything you can. You learn about the whole world, and you don't have to earn a living, pay the mortgage, or tend the babies.

But there's more than that. There's a great hidden payoff,

especially in tough subjects, even those in which you don't get A's or B's. If you have really done your best, you have learned to pay attention. You have had to pay attention to the teacher, to what the textbook said, and to doing the work as correctly as you could. You have sharpened your faculty of attention.

Earlier I said that your attention is a sign of love. You give your love to other people by the attention you pay them.

When you are older, there will be people who need your attention: your husband or wife, your children, your friends. The better the quality of attention you can give them, the better a spouse, parent, and friend you will be.

If you have learned how to pay attention in school, you have learned the greatest lesson of all. By learning how to focus totally on something, you have learned how to love!

When someone comes up to you with a problem, and you're thinking of what you have to do tomorrow, or what happened yesterday, or what you're going to do at lunchtime, or what somebody said to you the day before yesterday, or whether you're going to have a date for the dance next week, that person is not getting your love, because you are not giving full attention.

So to improve your schoolwork, you need to improve your ability to pay attention. That means when you're studying at home, turn off the TV and stereo. How can you read a book and watch TV? How can you hear the inner ring of the sentences in your mind if the music is on?

If you don't understand something in class, ask the teacher. That's a sign of intelligence. You are there to ask questions, to learn.

Always try to do a little extra on required assignments. Set aside a certain amount of time say, "I'm going to spend twenty minutes on this subject, twenty minutes on that subject, and twenty minutes on that other subject, and then my homework will be done." That way you save a lot of time worrying about doing your homework and dividing your attention.

Learning how to pay attention is a fantastic gift. That's what's wrong with the world: there aren't enough people who pay enough attention to other people. If you pay attention in class and to your homework assignments, you will have improved your grades but, more importantly, the quality of your life.

How much of my college education should I contribute to?

As much as you can, because it's your education. College costs an awful lot of money. Unless your parents are immensely wealthy, you, like many people, should help work your way through.

If you are capable of a college education you can get one. Every college has hundreds of scholarships available, based on need, or ability, or both. Most colleges have loan programs, and almost all offer students jobs on and off campus. To learn about these things, call or write the financial aid departments of whatever colleges you're interested in.

The more you help pay your own bills, the more you show your parents how dedicated you are to the pursuit of learning. Also, the less dependent you are on them, the more you are your own grown-up person.

I study, but I just can't get things to sink in. Then when report cards come around, I get C's and a few D's, and my parents get really mad. They won't believe I study, but I do—I just can't do well on tests. I get A's on all my daily work. How can I convince them that I understand everything and just do badly on tests?

It may not be so much a matter of convincing your parents as figuring out why you freeze up on tests.

First, show your parents your daily A work. That will put to rest any idea they might have that you're not doing your homework.

Then talk to one of your teachers and ask him or her how you can learn to take tests without tightening up. I suspect you're having a panic reaction when you take tests. You come in tense, and when the test is given, you blank out. You know the material, but you cannot show it on a test. A sympathetic teacher might give you some good pointers.

You might try reading a famous book called *The Relaxation Response,* by Herbert Benson, M.D. It teaches you a breathing exercise that can relax tension and help you center yourself. Yoga is another good habit to take up.

You want to stay cool and take the test as though it was any other thing. You have to talk and breathe yourself into that attitude. The moment you give a test such enormous importance in your life, you panic.

It might also help if you get together with a couple of other students and throw questions back and forth to one another before a test. Learn the material by heart, so when one of them throws a question at you, your answer comes fast. Then you throw a question at one of the others.

You can acclimate yourself to tests by taking "tests" in a context of friendship.

My mom says I'm addicted to video games, computers, and television. I guess I am. Why do kids get addicted to them? Are they bad? What can we do?

It's not that these things are bad or good; the problem is that if you spend too much time with video games you may be losing out on some of the more social aspects of life that you should be enjoying at this time.

Perhaps you are intentionally hiding out from those very social pursuits. Some kids do use computers and video games that way, because they are impersonal. You can stunt your social growth by doing that.

Try to taper down gradually. Limit yourself to an hour a day, or less, rather than going cold turkey. Games and computers are probably fun for you, and there's nothing wrong with a little recreation and fun. But try to limit how much time or money you spend. Learn to bowl or play chess with your friends. Read science fiction. Develop other talents.

Is it right to punish your kids for not getting good grades, even if they've tried?

No. As long as you're doing your best—doing your homework, and studying hard—there is no reason your parents should punish or discipline you. If they do, they're suggesting grades are more important than you are, and that's disastrous.

Some parents feel their egos are on the line when their children don't get good grades. I try to alert parents to that stupidity. They're not thinking of their childrens' welfare; they're only thinking of their own egos. The message you get is grades count, not you—and that's not true.

You have to make this clear to your parents. You may even ask your counselor at school to talk to them. Some people find academic work easier than others, but that doesn't mean they're worth more as people.

The stress teenagers feel about grades is already heavy. Parents adding to that stress by punishment are not helping at all. Show them this answer.

What do you think about old-fashioned, strict rules in schools that have modern kids?

I am certain your school has good reasons for its rules, which have probably been developed from dealing with thousands of students in an orderly fashion and in a way that provides a good atmosphere for learning.

No school administrator sits down and says, "I've decided that what we need is an old-fashioned, stupid rule" or "What we need is another dumb rule to interfere with the kids' happiness."

I, at least, have never met a school administrator who said, "What we've had to do is build up a bunch of crummy rules around here to see if we can't make these kids unhappy."

You might want to talk to your principal or one of your teachers if a specific rule bothers you so much. Find out what the motive behind the rule was. It may increase your understanding.

In my region, those schools that have gone back to basics, taken a "no nonsense" approach to schooling, have long lists of kids waiting to get in.

How can someone finish adolescence early in a society where an extensive education is needed to financially survive later on?

You imply you must be financially dependent on your parents throughout your college education. But that isn't true. As I have pointed out, you can find many alternative means of financing your education.

You end adolescence when you begin paying your own bills emotionally, financially, spiritually, and in every other way. When you stand on your own two feet, independent of your parents, you are through with adolescence.

To the extent you still say, "Well, I have to be financially dependent on my parents through college," you are still tied to them and haven't tried your own wings yet.

There's nothing wrong with that if your parents can afford it. But when you get to college you'll find there are people who are doing it on their own. They're not adolescents anymore. And they won't have to answer to their parents in certain ways, as you still will.

For instance, a wealthy attorney's son announced he needed extra money for college. The father sent it to him and then learned his son had used the money for a down payment on a sports car and was applying half his monthly allowance—intended for food and books—on the car payments.

The father promptly said, "There will be no more allowance." The kid went through the roof. But the father said, "If you want the car, you'll have to pay for it yourself. Or you'll have to sell it." Selling it is what the boy finally had to do. The student was still an adolescent dependent on his father for money. Consequently, his father had the parental right to decide how the money was spent.

Many young people are working their way through college, supplementing their own earnings with student loans or scholarships. Investigate. You may get out of adolescence faster than you had planned.

Did your children handle their problems with you the same way you're telling us to handle them with our parents?

I learned parenting skills as I went along. I did not necessarily handle the first of my children the way I did the eighth; I learned a lot in between.

But we always worked for open communication in our

family, and we always knew where we stood. My children didn't let me get away with much.

They were always free to bring up issues. And when my late wife or I saw one of our youngsters troubled by something, but not sharing it, we tried to initiate a discussion.

That goes on even now. When one of my sons or daughters visits me and I sense he or she is troubled by something. I'll invite him or her into my study and say, "Let's have a little chat. You appear troubled, is there anything you want to share with me?"(Now, however, the sharing is as equals and friends.)

Our boys and girls went through all the traumas boys and girls go through growing up. I am very proud of all of them, and I think that they're all friends of mine.

The last words any one of them ever hears from me are "I love you." That way, if my plane goes down, they will remember that their father's final words on the phone or in person were that I love them.

The love relationship is the most important in any family. Issues are less important.

Does life get easier as you get older?

Yes. Adolescence and puberty is a very stressful period. You are like a continent being formed by volcanic eruptions and fires. There are calm periods and then more eruptions. But despite all the stress, a continent truly is being formed.

You face the stresses of your body changing and of trying to identify who you are and what you want to be. You face the stresses of learning to relate to the opposite sex and of handling peer pressures about drugs, booze, and sex. And all the while you have pressures in school.

Later, of course, you will encounter different stresses, because there's no such thing as life without stress. But you'll be able to cope more maturely. You'll be more realistic about yourself and the world.

But even so, it takes most people about forty years to discover the map is not the territory. Aristotle, for example, said it takes forty years to be a philosopher. Thomas Aquinas, one of the great thinkers of the Middle Ages, agreed.

What they meant was that as we gain experience dealing with life and all kinds of people (not just the narrow world of our family and friends), we learn to accept responsibility for ourselves.

At that point—about age forty—we begin to take another look at our values. We begin to see that reality may not be what we thought it was when we were eighteen.

Then, finally, we can let go of some baggage.

We learn grudges are useless and only harm us, that holding onto anger gives us ulcers. We learn how to love more unselfishly. One of the great things family life teaches us is to be unselfish. As husband and wife, as parents, we have to share our lives, our livelihoods, our resources, our time, our attention.

We continue learning all those things, and they slowly become easier.

Just as once it was difficult for you to tie your shoes but today it's a snap, by the time you're forty you'll automatically be doing loving things for your family or friends—things that you were too self-conscious to do when you were sixteen or seventeen.

As you mature, you learn how your parents influenced who you are. You begin to see how wise they were in some things. Mark Twain said that when he was seventeen his father was the stupidest man on earth; when he reached twenty-three, he was astonished at how much his father had learned in six years.

It takes time, but eventually we learn how wise our parents were to protect us from some things, and how well-meaning they were even when they mishandled things.

I'll put it another way:

At the age of ninety, the painter Pablo Picasso had a retrospective exhibit showing his lifetime of work. He had started with dark, moody painting like Rembrandt and then moved into his Blue Period. His art was still realistic and gauzy. Then he went through his Pink Period, emphasizing pinks and somewhat realistic images. Finally he went into periods of fauvism and cubism, marked by great energy and frenetic images—a whole different way of looking at reality. It was a breakthrough in art that influenced modern design.

And then Picasso entered his great peak. He painted *Guernica*—a huge, powerful antiwar statement—and explored African art forms. He allowed himself to be influence by Cro-Magnon cave paintings, began sketching simple designs of bulls, bison, and antelope and doing pottery pieces that were playful and almost childlike.

A gentleman toured the exhibit and went up to Picasso. He said, "Señor Picasso, this whole exhibit should be reversed. The playful, childlike things that you've been doing lately should be first; then should come those lovely, stylized, almost primitive figures of horses and bison; then, the erotic pictures; then the powerful *Guernica;* then the abstractions; then the rosy period of late autumn; then the blues of early winter; and finally, the somber tones of old age—in short, the reverse of what you have here."

Picasso is reputed to have laughed, rumbled, and then laughed again. He said, "Oh no, Señor, you are very wrong; it takes a long time to grow young."

He was right.

Many people are almost on their deathbed before they

learn how to live, before they really appreciate that today is not preparation for life—today *is* life.

The quality of your life today is determined by how you relate to your parents, brothers and sisters, and friends in school.

If your relationships are painful, you should work to change yourself and make them less painful. You should work to change how you relate to yourself and make that less painful, too. You are not meant to be marking time waiting for the future but living creatively and lovingly right now.

Unfortunately, most of us learn those simple lessons the hard way, though life experience.

And when we finally do learn them, life gets easier.

Selected Reading

Benson, Herbert. *The Relaxation Response.* New York: Avon Books, 1975.

Bozarth-Campbell, Alla. *Life is Goodbye, Life is Hello: Grieving Well Through All Kinds of Loss.* Minneapolis: CompCare, 1982.

Colgrove, Melba, Harold Bloomfield, and Peter McWilliams. *How to Survive the Loss of a Love.* New York: Signet, 1976.

Jampolsky, Gerald. *Love is Letting Go of Fear.* New York: Bantam, 1970.

Kushner, Harold. *When Bad Things Happen to Good People.* New York: Avon Books, 1981.

Procaccini, Joseph and Mark W. Kiefaber. *P.L.U.S. Parenting.* New York: Doubleday and Company, Inc., 1985.

Short, Ray E. *Sex, Love or Infatuation: How Can I Really Know?* Minneapolis: Augsburg, 1978.